Typing Three
An Advanced Course

Typing Three
An Advanced Course

Joanna Gaukroger

Head of School, Business and Secretarial Studies
Gloucestershire College of Arts and Technology

Archie Drummond

and

Anne Coles-Mogford

Oxford and County Secretarial College

McGRAW-HILL BOOK COMPANY

London · New York · St Louis · San Francisco · Auckland · Bogotá · Guatemala
Hamburg · Lisbon · Madrid · Mexico · Montreal · New Delhi · Panama · Paris
San Juan · São Paulo · Singapore · Sydney · Tokyo · Toronto

Published by
McGRAW-HILL Book Company (UK) Limited
SHOPPENHANGERS ROAD · MAIDENHEAD · BERKSHIRE · ENGLAND
TEL: 0628-23432 FAX: 0628-35895

British Library Cataloguing in Publication Data

Gaukroger, Joanna
Typing three.
1. Typing
I. Title II. Drummond, A. M. (Archibald Manson) *1924–*
III. Coles-Mogford, Anne
652.3

ISBN 0-07-707270-7

Library of Congress Cataloging-in-Publication Data

Gaukroger, Joanna.
Typing three: an advanced course / Joanna Gaukroger, Archie Drummond, and Anne Coles-Mogford
p. cm.
ISBN 0-07-707270-7
1. Typewriting. I. Drummond, Archie. II. Coles-Mogford, Anne. III. Title.
Z49.G34 1990 90-32594
652.3'026—dc20 CIP

1 2 3 4 5 NI 9 3 2 1 0

Typeset by Eta Services (Typesetters) Ltd, Beccles, Suffolk
Printed and bound in Italy by New Interlitho

INDEX TO CONTENTS

PREFACE

Advanced technology is making it practical for business people to work from their cars, from aeroplanes, from hotel rooms and, of course, from home.

They will have:

their machines to transmit facsimile documents;
their car telephones linked to their electronic offices;
their personal computers sending messages around the world by satellite;
their Qwerty keyboard and function keys with which to receive and despatch vast amounts of information.

Therefore, to meet the changes being brought about by the effect of technology on office work, you must not only have the confidence and ability to produce neatly typed and mailable transcripts, but must also develop proficiency in certain skills that will make you more employable and give you greater opportunity for promotion in the electronic office.

A new vocabulary has evolved with the development of electronic machines, and the efficient typist must be highly skilled in proofreading and editing for accuracy in word usage, spelling, punctuation and grammar.

As an **advanced** typist, you should have a high degree of proficiency in typing, an understanding of a wide range of business documents, and be skilled in the presentation of clean, mailable copies without error and within a given time, together with the ability to deal adequately with the rearrangement and typing of tabulation, statistical and technical reports, forms, lists, etc.

The advanced typist seeking employment with responsibility or looking for promotion should have:

1 the ability to use materials and time economically and effectively;
2 the ingenuity to organize the workload and workstation for greater efficiency;
3 the confidence to manage the obligations of responsibility and authority;
4 the expertise to manipulate skilfully the keyboards and the various devices found on computers, word processors and electronic typewriters;
5 a clear understanding of the concepts and applications of the automated office.

This text has been designed to give you a high degree of success in meeting the objectives outlined above: it offers the advanced typist a comprehensive and modern typewriting programme and will meet the needs of candidates for any Stage III typewriting examination and for:

the LCCI Private Secretary's Certificate and Private and Executive Secretary's Diploma;
the RSA Diploma for Personal Assistants and Teacher's Certificate in Typewriting;
the Typewriting Teachers' Diploma of the Joint Examining Board;
the City and Guilds Further Education Teachers' Certificate and Inservice Course for Teachers.

While your aim, no doubt, is to gain an examination certificate, we have also kept well to the fore the needs of business, and many exercises are based on material, layout and standards required by an employer. However, we would mention that while this textbook gives the best advice on layout and exercises that are possible after a great deal of research into office requirements and examiner's needs, you may find that your employer, or examiner will ask you to display a document in a slightly different style from that given in the textbook. An employer and an examiner may, for a great variety of reasons, require certain matter to be set out in what could be considered an unusual style. But that is their prerogative! In such instances, follow the layout of a previously typed document or follow instructions. In business, you must conform to the wishes of your employer; in an examination you follow instructions. In both, you must be consistent in layout, spelling, punctuation, use of words and figures, etc.

Skill building

In order to be able to carry out the varied kinds of typing required in an office, or in an examination, you will have to improve your basic typing power, and this section provides a consistent review of the typing and machine techniques that will increase speed and improve accuracy. The skill building pages contain intensive drills on:

1 (a) alphabetic sentences, figures and symbols, double-letter consonants, common prefixes and suffixes, single-hand words, common abbreviations, roman numerals, word building, foreign currencies, etc;
(b) **language arts skills** spelling [before typing the drill, find the word(s) misspelt and make a note of any word(s) that cause you difficulty and type it (them) at every available opportunity] proofreading, apostrophe, subject/verb agreement;

2 **skill measurement** As only you or your teacher will know whether, at any given time, you should be practising for speed or accuracy, we have called the speed/accuracy material skill measurement, and a choice must be made as to whether the practice should aim at increasing speed or working for greater accuracy. In unit 1 and then each alternate

unit, there are one-minute skill measurement exercises ranging from 44 to 74 wpm.

In addition, there are five, one-page timed skill measurement exercises;

3 **production development** Starting with unit 2 and in each alternate unit, there are short, timed production development exercises to be typed from manuscript. In order to increase your skill in working from amended manuscript, you should work on these exercises extensively, always striving to produce them faster and more accurately.

Production skill

Both speed and accuracy are components of production skill, and the documents in this textbook provide a thorough review of all machine and typing techniques and develop them to the higher levels required for fast and accurate production; also covered are the theory and conventions that you will need for instant decisions in order that you may complete a particular task accurately and within a given time. In business, you must follow the house style preferred by your employer; in examinations, you should follow the layout and instructions—if neither is given, follow the typewriting conventions in this textbook. Candidates taking the advanced stage of any typing examination should be capable of using any style of display.

The course moves gradually from the very simple to the complex and you will have to:

take decisions and make judgements—paper, margins display, etc;
follow oral and written instructions;
abstract information and details from unorganized sources;
copy information from previously completed tasks;
compose correspondence from notes.

Integrated production typing

Our objective here is to simulate typical office typing, and the tasks are preceded by a **typist's log sheet** which gives the name of the organization, the originator's name and department, additional directions for operators using word processors, text-editing electronic typewriters and correction only electronic typewriters. For further details about timing, folders, mailable documents, etc, please read pages 24 and 25.

Word processing procedures

Although you may not have access to word processors, electronic typewriters and computers with word processing capabilities, you should take every opportunity to familiarize yourself with the terminology. We have included word processing and data processing terminology throughout the text, and wherever we considered it appropriate we have mentioned word processing concepts and applications that would apply to the operations being practised. We hope these points will enable you to prepare more fully for the electronic office. Further, we have suggested certain tasks that may be used as **input**, and **text editing changes** are listed separately.

Data files

These are on pages 102–103 and, from the details listed under a **filename**, you have to select information to complete certain exercises (names, addresses, prices, standard paragraphs, etc).

Data bank

This section contains all the theory and typewriting conventions that have been acceptable practice over the years.
It is important that you turn to the page stated and read the appropriate section if you are unsure about how the particular exercise should be displayed.

Workguide and Resource Material

In the end section of the *Workguide and Resource Material* for *Typing: Two-and-One Course, Second Edition* are suggested layouts for the exercises in *Typing Three*. When you have typed an exercise, compare it with the solution and note any differences, taking care to see that you have carried out all the instructions. It also contains letterhead paper, forms, etc, which may be duplicated and which will make your typing much more meaningful.

Acknowledgements

We sincerely thank our colleagues for their valuable help and suggestions as well as for assisting with the copying of the manuscript work.

The pages that follow will give you a comprehensive and complete coverage of typewriting conventions and practice, together with sufficient information to help you to understand word processing terminology and techniques, and we hope that this will give you a sound basis on which to build your future. We see the electronic office as an absorbing and stimulating place in which to work—a place of change and challenge—and if you are both flexible and receptive to change, and willing to adapt to new office equipment, your future would seem assured. We wish you well and hope that your expertise will bring you satisfaction and a rich reward.

Joanna Gaukroger
Archie Drummond
Anne Coles-Mogford

INTRODUCTION

To make sure you understand the objectives you have to aim for, you must read this introduction (and the preface) and refer to it from time to time.

Guide to document presentation

Over the years, certain conventions with regard to display and layout of typewritten documents have become accepted practice. While examining bodies and employers do not now worry unduly about layout as long as the document is clean, attractive and correct (no typing, spelling, or grammatical errors), we do suggest that you use the 'theory' conventions given in this textbook as a guide.

There is no one correct style of layout for any typed document. In a business letter, there is no reason why you should leave only one clear space between the different parts before the salutation; a short letter will look more attractive if you leave two or even three spaces, but be consistent! However, it would be ridiculous to turn up six single spaces between the parts. In any situation, where **specific instructions** are given, these must be followed precisely.

Employment

Many employers will be adamant about how a particular document should be displayed, because a uniform style increases efficiency and reduces costs. If there are few variations in style, the mechanics of typing become automatic. Also, most electronic machines and word processors have preset margins which, if desired, need not be changed. The advantage of **uniformity** is obvious: a consistent style does not call attention to itself but enables the reader to concentrate on the meaning. Be consistent with spelling and the use of capitals. Do not type an abbreviation in one paragraph and then type the same abbreviation in full in the next paragraph. Also, be consistent in the use of words and figures, open and full punctuation, style of headings and enumeration.

If your employer does not indicate a house style, or give you a specific format, then you are more or less free to use your own initiative, but the nearer your layout and style are to what is considered appropriate display (mainly based on typewriting conventions) the more acceptable the finished document is likely to be.

Examinations

Examiners are allowing greater latitude in the layout used by candidates, and this is to be welcomed.

Certain examining bodies insist that candidates must attempt each task; otherwise, they fail the examination. This means that examination candidates should not be indecisive about formatting and typing documents, and, in the absence of specific instructions, must be able to complete the work with confidence. We suggest that the necessary self-assurance, theoretical knowledge and practice can be acquired only by following a particular course of training which offers the fundamentals, the necessary refinements, and speed plus accuracy to prepare the typist for an advanced examination and a responsible post. *Typing Three: An Advanced Course* offers the typist exactly this type of training.

Language arts

In business today, and more so in the electronic office of tomorrow, typists must be proficient in the application of English language skills and have a comprehensive knowledge of modern business technology. Typists taking an advanced typewriting examination, or seeking a post of responsibility, should:

1 have a good knowledge of words and their meanings
2 know how to spell correctly;
3 know how to form plurals, compound words and possessives;
4 know how to punctuate.

We all find difficulty in **spelling** certain words and to help you overcome some of the more common spelling errors, we have included spelling drills in the skill building pages. When typing these words, pay particular attention to the sequence of letters and make a note of words that cause you difficulty. Also included are drills on the use of the **apostrophe** and **agreement** of subject and verb.

Word errors (spelling errors, typing errors, wrong use of the apostrophe, etc) are included in a number of exercises in this textbook. **You must find and correct the word errors that occur in all units.**

Workstation

A workstation is defined as the place where an employee performs his/her office tasks, and the object of the modern workstation is to help the individual increase productivity. However, the most up-to-date workstation will not in itself increase your output if you do not have all your needs to hand and, at the same time, make good use of today's office aids, furnishings and machines.

Arranging your workstation carefully will not only help to increase your output; in addition, it will give you a more comfortable and pleasant workplace. Reserve the top of your desk for the materials you will use constantly. At all times you must have quick access to:

note pad, telephone message forms;
all types of stationery (bond paper for top copies, bank paper for carbon copies) including envelopes, labels and carbon paper;
pens, pencils, rulers, correction paper/fluid/eraser, paper clips (a tray with built-in dividers is indispensable for these items);
reference materials: dictionary, calendar, telephone directory, telephone index, office reference manual, pocket-sized calculator, etc;
personal items should be kept at the back of a bottom drawer;
items normally kept inside drawers, or on shelves, should be returned immediately after use;
disks should be stored upright (not stacked) and **must** be returned to the disk file when no longer required and particularly at the end of the day; keep related disks together—perhaps a disk-file box for commercial software, another for current work, and yet another for seldom-used disks.

Posture

A suitable **chair** is essential—not only for your work, but also for your health. You should adjust your chair to meet your personal needs by changing the angle, height and tension of the back support as well as the height of the seat. **Good posture** is of paramount importance. Keep your:

feet flat on the floor;
arms and **elbows** hanging loosely,
back straight;
fingers slightly curved;
body centred on the letter J;
forearms same slope as keyboard.

Do not sit rigidly still as this will increase the pressure on your spine—flex, twist and stretch regularly.

VDU screen

Wherever possible:

1 position the body so that you are looking straight ahead at the VDU—avoid looking at the screen sideways;
2 lean forward from the hips—do not bend your shoulders;
3 eyes level with the top of the screen and between 16 and 30 inches from the screen;
4 use adequate lighting and see that there is no glare on the screen from daylight or artificial light.

Electronic typewriters and word processors

This is the symbol that we will use to draw your attention to information and instructions for **electronic typewriters** and **word processors**. In business today, it is important that you understand how these machines may be employed to format more easily a great variety of documents.

The text editing instructions are given on pages 100 and 101. In the top right-hand corner of the hard copy, write the filename and keep all the hard copies in alphabetical order (according to the filename) in a folder.

the correction key and the correct character is inserted.

The checked and corrected typing is transferred to the permanent memory by pressing a particular function key, and the printout of the document on the screen takes place when the print key is pressed.

Window envelopes

Some firms use envelopes from which a panel has been cut out at the front. This is known as a 'window' envelope. The object of window envelopes is twofold:

1 It saves time in typing the name and address on both letter and envelope.
2 It avoids the possibility of error in copying the address on the envelope.

When a window envelope is used, the name and address of the addressee must be typed in full on the letter itself, and in such a position that, when the letter is folded, the position of the address will coincide with the cut-out portion on the envelope. To help the typist, the position of the cut-out is sometimes marked on the letter heading either by marks in the corner or by a ruled box. Window envelopes may also be provided with a transparent cover over the cut-out part.

This type of envelope is not normally used for personal letters. It is used, without the transparent cover, mainly for statements, invoices, form letters, etc.

Words and figures

1 Use words instead of figures for:
  1.1 The number one on its own.*
  1.2 Figures at the beginning of a sentence.
2 Use figures in all other cases.

* If number one is part of a list of figures, it should be typed as a figure, eg 'Follow the instructions in 1, 2 and 3'.

NOTE: These are the basic rules, but other methods may be used.

Workstation

See page viii.

SKILL BUILDING 1

1 Alphabetic sentences Type each sentence twice

A sizeable amount of time was spent on various sports including boxing, squash, judo and hockey.

She acquired another glass of fizzy lemon juice from the takeaway bar over the wool shop.

2 Improve control of words using the main double-letter consonants (C, D, F, L, M, P, R, S, T)

accessible successful occasion accounts accurate acceptance

sudden additional addressee addendum hidden middle forbidden

offered different difficult effective affected effort suffer

challenge travelling excellent following fulfilling alleviate

commercial immediately imminent commitment committee programme

disappoint disappear appreciate application supply apparently

occurrence narrow arrive deterrent error arrear arrangement

business assess assistant possible excessive dismissal possess

latter matter letter better attention pattern attractive

3 Practise typing superscripts/subscripts

H_2SO_4 m^2 note^1 250 ^oC $x^2(9y^2 + x^2y^2 + 3x)^5$ ± §

4 Skill measurement Target time for each exercise is 1 minute, not more than 1 error.

Quality clothing manufacturers of all sizes across the UK take space at the annual Midlands' menswear exhibition. Companies take the opportunity to demonstrate new products to top customers from a wide geographical area.

220 keystrokes (44 words)

A nun was refused service at a café because she pulled up on a motorbike. The owner said 'Sorry, we don't serve bikers!' The sister replied 'What do you think a middle-aged lady is going to do - take the place apart?'

220 keystrokes (44 words)

NOTE: The underscore in totals must extend from the first figure to the last figure as in the example below.

```
                              £

                          1,643
                          2,456
Do not turn up →          1,021
                          -----
Turn up two spaces →
                         £5,120
Turn up one space →      ======
```

Typeface styles

See also ***Pitch***, page 134.
In addition to the standard pica and elite, a wide selection of typefaces (styles and sizes) is available—italic, script, extra light or dark faces and a number of others.

International typefaces (German, French, Spanish, etc) are also available.

Typing from print

Today, most firms keep on hand a wide variety of type sizes and styles for use in typing documents of all kinds and especially for preparing camera-ready copy (CRC). The increasing use of electronic keyboards and other sophisticated machines now available for desktop publishing, means that many organizations print their own circulars, leaflets and catalogues. When copying from print, make judicious use of the following in order to effect more eye-catching headings, subheadings, etc.

1 Where a word(s) is in italic print, underline the word when typing.
2 Where a word(s) needs to be emphasized, use bold face, underscore (not if you are already using the underscore for italic print) or closed capitals.
3 Main heading in spaced capitals three spaces between words with/without underscore/bold face.
4 Subheading in closed capitals with one or two spaces between words, with/without underscore/bold face.
5 Other subsidiary headings: Initial capital(s) and lower case letters with/without underscore/bold face.
6 Shoulder headings and paragraph headings with/without underscore/bold face.

Consider the relative value of the various headings before you start typing and place the emphasis accordingly. For the sake of clarity and smooth continuity, you must be economical in the use of any one form of emphasis; otherwise, the value of that method will be lost.

Typing on reverse side of paper

See ***Reverse side of paper***, page 141.

Typist's log sheet

See page 24.

Variable linespacer

You will find the variable linespacer (sometimes called cylinder release) on the left cylinder knob. By pressing in (or pulling out on some machines) the variable linespacer, you release the spacing mechanism, and the cylinder can be moved to any desired position.

It is used for:
Filling in form letters.
Typing on ruled lines.
Finding the correct alignment when paper has been reinserted to make a correction.

Variables

Items that differ from one to another. See ***Forms***, page 123, ***Form letters***, page 123, and ***Standard paragraphs***, page 144.

Vertical display

See ***Display***, page 116.

Visual display unit

A great many electronic machines now have an attachment called a visual display unit (sometimes referred to as a cathode-ray tube (CRT)). This is a screen, similar to a television screen, on which you can see exactly what you have typed. While the typing is on the screen, alterations and amendments may be made. The typist moves the cursor (a moving marker which indicates to the typist the point at which the next character may be typed) across the screen to a mistake, the correction is typed over the mistake and the memory may or may not be corrected at the same time, or the wrong character is erased by

Exercise 1

Type the following letter to Neil Cooke (Roofing) Ltd. Use two-thirds A4 Goring District Council headed paper (see *Workguide and Resource Material*) and type the address at the foot of the letter, as shown.

Ref. PL/RD44022

N. P. COOKE

FOR THE ATTENTION OF MR ~~B T THORNTON~~

Dear Sir,

422

A/C NO. D/~~224~~/927

400 On checking my records, it has become aparent that the sum of £~~250.14~~ has been credited to your a/c in error.

improving

This has had the unfxortunate effect of ~~increasing~~ the balance shown on your a/c. The credit note for £~~44.57~~, despatched on ~~5 June~~ shd have been £~~33.67~~. I enclose a revised statexxment indicating the true position. £566.26 (966.26)

Please accept our apologies for this unfortunate occurrence.

Yours faithfully,

(typist - 1st Friday of last mth, please insert date)

Borough Treasurer

Thornton Newell & Associates
Tower House,
Watling Street Road,
BIRMINGHAM.
B4 6YB

(address in DataFiles, filename ALPHA, page 102)

Exercise 2

Type the following letter on two-thirds A4 Goring District Council headed paper (see *Workguide and Resource Material*). Type the address at the foot of the letter, as in exercise 1.

from Borough Treasurer to Robert Howell (address in DataFiles, filename ALPHA, page 102.)

I enclose yr salary check & payslip relating to this mth. [Many members of staff have asked me to pass on their good wishes.]

We do hope th you make a rapid recovery & return to us before ~~too~~ long. (MARK REGISTERED) Ref RH/Per/90

(Do not type salutation & complimentary close. Leave suff space as I wish to handwrite them.)

Telex message

In the United Kingdom the telex system is fully automatic and immediate connection is made by direct dialling to any subscriber. Similarly, many subscribers in Europe and beyond may be obtained by direct dialling. Therefore, when preparing a telex message, the typist should include the receiver's telex number to save the teleprinter operator's time when despatching the message. The sender's name and telex number will appear at the end of the message.

Organizations with teleprinter facilities usually have their own design of telex form on which the typist will type a telex message which is then passed to the teleprinter operator.

The advantage of a telex message is that both sender and receiver have an immediate copy of the message, and there is no possibility of misunderstanding, as may be the case when the telephone is used. Further, there is no need to send a letter of confirmation.

Text-editing machines (word processors, computers, electronic typewriters)

Specialists who studied the work done by office typists found that a great deal of time was spent in retyping documents that had been slightly altered, or retyping documents that required only minor alterations in wording and layout. As a result of this research, text-editing machines were designed with storage and revision capabilities.

They are automated pieces of equipment (with QWERTY keyboards and function keys) on which the material is typed and recorded on some form of medium for playback or for correction; therefore, text editing refers to the revision of documents that have already been recorded. The machines may use magnetic tape, magnetic card or (more common) magnetic disk (floppy disk or diskette) as a recording media.

Some text-editing machines have a 'temporary' memory, which means that if the machine is turned off, the matter just typed will be lost. Other machines will retain matter for a certain period of time. The more complex machines can be instructed to transfer the typing to 'permanent' memory or external storage.

When using a text-editing machine, typing errors no longer cause difficulty. Most have a simple backspace-strikeover sequence (backspace and strike the correct character over the error) to correct an error. When revising or reformatting text, it is possible, on the more sophisticated machines, to move a page, paragraphs or sentences from one section of a document to another.

We would like to emphasize that although the correction of errors is very simple on text-editing machines, it is still time-consuming, and accurate typing in the first instance is imperative.

The type font (all the characters in a particular type style) may be a golf ball head or a daisywheel and the font may be changed at any time while typing on an electronic machine, thus enabling the typist to give emphasis or style to a particular piece of typing—large typeface for main headings, pica typeface for subheadings, italic typeface to emphasize particular words, etc.

Time

1 Twenty-four hour clock

As international travel has become more popular, we are all more aware of the 24-hour clock. It always consists of four figures with no full stops; for example:

0001 hours (one minute after midnight) 0700 hours (7.00 am) 1200 hours (noon) 1300 hours (1.00 pm) 1800 hours (6.00 pm) 2359 hours (11.59 pm). Midnight is always represented by the word 'midnight'.

2 am/pm and o'clock

Words or figures may be used with o'clock: one o'clock, 9 o'clock. Use **am** and **pm** with figures with no space between the two letters; see examples above. There is a full stop after each letter when using full punctuation, eg 4.00 p.m.

Totals

When typing totals proceed as follows:

1 Type the underscore for the first line above the total. **Do not** turn up before typing this line.
2 Turn up twice and type the total.
3 Turn up once and type the line below the total.
4 Turn the cylinder up slightly by using the interliner lever and type the second line. Then return the interliner to its normal position.

Exercise 3

Type the following letter on A4 Grant Archer headed paper (see *Workguide and Resource Material*). Head your second page with the page number, today's date and Graham Vernon, on separate lines in double spacing.

from George Parkinson to Graham Vernon

top + 3 please

cc Neil Willis

bcc Michael Devlin

REF RL/TU/typist's initials

Dr Graham — Exhibition Stand - The Money Show

~~Many thanks~~ Thank you v much for ~~yr~~ the model & the designs wh you produced ~~from~~ for our new stand at The Money Show on ~~5-9 Aug~~ 25-27 Apr (typist insert yr).

We have carefully considered all the proposals submitted & I am pleased to tell you that ~~we fe~~ feel that yr overall 'package' wl prove the most successful. We shd, therefore, like to award you the contract.

On the basis of yr quoted daily rate, we ~~have estimated~~ calculate yr charges for the project to be: (typist please insert the charges shown overleaf)

~~We wl~~ both Neil Willis & I sh be resp for the costs of all construction materials, transport & payment of subcontractors. Please inform me if you envisage exceeding these/subs/ allocations by more than 10%.

There is 1 significant change to our original proposals. Due to a withdrawal we have been able to secure a better sight in the form of Stand No E36 in Hall B, giving us a frontage of 10m & an overall stand size of 10m x 7.65m. All other measurements are as previously advised. Of yr 2 colour ~~schemes~~ choices we wd prefer the deep wine/white colour scheme to the navy/white.

We sh be working to a tight schedule, & it is essential th all parties adhere strictly to the deadline dates already advised. (insert 1 here) Neil wl be resp for managing the contract on our side. He wl be in touch before the end of the wk to arrange the 1st of our liaison meetings.

(1) Any unforseen sources of difficulty ~~shd~~ must be flagged immed they occur so th we can consider the knock-on affects against our other activities & make ~~any~~ adjustments accordingly.

Graham Vernon's address is in the DataFile, filename ALPHA, page 102.

12 *Rearrangement of tabular matter*

12.1 It is often necessary to rearrange the matter. Before starting to type, it is essential that you make a rough plan of what has to be done.

12.2 When columns in tabulation are very wide, it is necessary to consider where space can be saved. The following hints will be of help to you in such cases.

- 12.2.1 If the longest lines of the columns are in the headings, additional lines may be taken for these, so as to reduce the width required for the columns.
- 12.2.2 If the longest lines are in the descriptive column, the length of these lines may be reduced by taking extra lines for lengthy items. If this is done, allowance must be made for these extra lines when calculating the number of vertical lines required.
- 12.2.3 As a last resort, you may have to leave one space only between vertically ruled columns or a minimum of two spaces between unruled columns.
- 12.2.4 To save vertical spaces, it may be necessary to omit spaces before and after horizontal lines, or to use halfspacing before and after these lines.
- 12.2.5 In any one piece of typing the same number of spaces must be left between the widest item of each column.

Tailpiece

This is an illustration or ornamental motif at the end of a page, unit or chapter and is made up by combining characters, such as hyphen, colon, etc.

```
: -: -: -: -: -:
  -: -: -: -: -
    : -: -: -:
      -: -: -
        : -:
          -
```

Telephone index

It is usual to keep a list of names and addresses and telephone numbers that are frequently required. For this purpose, use is made of the strip-indexing method whereby each name and address and telephone number are typed on a separate strip. The strips are usually supplied in sheets, and the details are typed on the strips which are afterwards separated from the sheet. They are then inserted alphabetically in devices or frames specially made to take them. These strips can be moved up or down to allow additional strips to be inserted in their correct order, or to remove strips containing obsolete names. The surname is usually typed first, in upper case letters, followed by the initial(s) and then the address, all on one line if possible. If two lines are needed, these must be in single spacing as the strip is usually not more than 6 mm in depth. In order to carry the eye from the end of the address to the telephone number, continuous dots may be inserted leaving one clear space before the first dot and one clear space after the last dot.

NOTE: In an index or alphabetical list a comma is typed after the surname and after the initials. In the example below it will be seen that the right margin has been aligned.

Open punctuation

BROWN, A J, 46 Thomas Street, Leeds LS2 9JT 0532 21375
FISHER, L, & Co Ltd, 20 Clitton Road, Northampton NN1 5BQ 0604 6868

Full punctuation

BROWN, A. J., 46 Thomas Street, Leeds. LS2 9JT 0532 21375
FISHER, L., & Co. Ltd., 20 Clitton Road, Northampton. NN1 5BQ 0604 6868

Exercise 3 *(continued)*

If you wish to speak to him before then, his tel no is Warwick (typist add from Data Files, filename ALPHA, page 102). [I look forward to a successfull Money Show!

~~Best~~ Best wishes

Yrs sin — —

CP
PR Manager

PS - Can you advice Michael Devlin, our A/cs Manager, on yr VAT position?

(details of charges to be inserted overleaf)

	£
15 days' work @ £350 per day	5250.00
travel & subsistence (approx 15 X £30)	450.00
misc draughting materials	100.00
	5800.00

Exercise 4

Type the following draft telex message in capital letters throughout. Omit any accents on the capitals.

TELEX TO: SPECTRA GMBH, DARMSTADT, WEST GERMANY

" NO: 57884 (SPEC G)

(use A5 landscape paper please)

FAO: FRANS PORTIELJE

We hve booked the ARDEN HOTEL, BIRMINGHAM for yr visit to THE MONEY SHOW on (typist insert dates from para 1 of the letter to Graham ~~Vern~~ Vernon). (Please confirm) yr travelling arrangements ~~asap~~ by return.

Regards JACK BERREN.

tens under tens, etc. Centre the hyphen where there are no figures given.

6.12 Turn up one single space before inserting the last horizontal line and mark the points at which the vertical lines will be placed.

7 Subdivided column headings–blocked style

If you use blocked-style tabulation, then it is not necessary to centre subdivided headings vertically or horizontally. Starting points for headings will be the left margin and the tab stops for each column. Each column heading will start on the same horizontal line which will be the starting point for the deepest heading.

8 Columns of figures

In columns of figures, care must be taken to see that units are typed under units, tens under tens, etc. When figures are in thousands and above, you may leave a space between hundreds and thousands, thousands and millions or you may put in a comma, eg 1,326,978; 793,220; or 1 326 978; 793 220.

9 Reference signs and footnotes

Tabular work frequently has footnotes to explain some reference to the figures or details in the table. The same points apply to these footnotes and their corresponding reference signs in the body of the tables as those already explained for manuscript work, ie the footnotes are typed underneath the table in single spacing with double spacing between each. The reference sign in the body is typed immediately after the item to which it refers and is always a superscript. In the footnote, the sign may be typed either on the same line or as a superscript, and one space is left after the sign and before the start of the typing.

It should be noted that when you use the asterisk on the keyboard (not a combination character of x and hyphen) then the sign will be a superscript and any other footnote signs used in the same exercise must be superscripts. Usually there is no ruled line before a footnote in tabulation.

10 Vertical column headings

Headings to the columns may be typed vertically, either for emphasis or because of lack of space.

To find the number of linespaces to be left between the first and second horizontal lines to allow for the vertical headings, count the number of character spaces in the longest line of the heading and add three extra character spaces (one before and one after the longest line, and one for the second horizontal line). If you are using 12 pitch, divide this number by two to find how many spaces to leave for the headings. For example: longest line contains 11 characters $+3 = 14 \div 2 = 7$. Type the first horizontal line, turn up seven single spaces and type the second horizontal line. If you are using 10 pitch, the calculation is more complicated, and we suggest that you type the longest heading on a piece of paper and measure, with a ruler, the space occupied.

Complete the tabulation and rule before reinserting the paper into the typewriter lengthways. Type the vertical headings. It is usual for all headings to start at the point fixed for the longest heading, even if the tabulation is typed in the centred style of display. The headings will be centred between the two vertical lines.

If the headings are typed downwards, they can be typed first with each letter of the heading typed one under the other and the ruling completed in the usual way.

11 Oblique column headings

Headings to the columns may be typed obliquely, usually for greater emphasis.

To type oblique headings it will be necessary to insert the paper into the typewriter diagonally, as the headings must be typed parallel to the oblique lines and centred between the two. Rule the table and, when the paper is reinserted, type the headings, the oblique lines being aligned with the alignment scale.

The scale points for these lines must be marked in pencil and the following procedure should be adopted:

11.1 In the usual way, find the horizontal spaces required for the column items and the spaces between the columns. Rule the first horizontal line, but add one extra column, ie if the longest line in the column is three, and three spaces have been left between the columns, then add six extra spaces to the first horizontal line.

11.2 Find the number of vertical spaces required for the headings in the same way as for vertical headings (see 10 opposite). Leave the required number of spaces and rule the second horizontal line in the usual way.

11.3 Along the second line, mark in pencil the scale points for the vertical lines between columns (which will also be the scale points for the **bottom** of the oblique lines), and set tab stops for the start of each column as usual.

11.4 Mark the scale points for the **top** of the oblique lines as follows:

11.4.1 The top of the first oblique line should be marked at the same scale point as the second vertical line, the top of the second oblique line at the same scale point as the third vertical line, etc.

Exercise 5

Type the following memo on A5 headed memo paper (see *Workguide and Resource Material*).

Memo from Nicholas Ridley to All departmental managers.

Auditors ← (emphasize heading) CONFIDENTIAL

The internal auditors [(insert 1)] have informed me that they wl be paying us a visit, week commencing (typist-plse insert 2nd Monday of next month). [~~Mr Bray has expressed his concern about certain irregularities in the operation of our devolved petty cash system~~. He wl doubtless wish to examine this a/c in detail, & discuss the matter w anyone directly concerned.

Please make sure that all recs and associated paperwork are ~~available~~ assembled in good time. (1) John Bray & Sheila Wallis

Circulation: (alphabetically)

T. Walker, R. Rose, R. Bray, S. Appleton, M. Pinter (add Christian names from Datafiles, ALPHA, page 102)

Ref: NR/yr initials

Prepare a skeleton memo form and embolden all the headings (including the word memorandum) and save under filename MEMO. Recall the form and use for exercise 5 above and for all other memoranda where appropriate.

Exercise 6

Type the following memo on A5 headed memo paper (see *Workguide and Resource Material*).

Memo from Barry Hunt to Karen Jones (designations in DataFiles, ALPHA, page 102.)

NEWPORT WORKS At there meeting ~~today~~ yesterday, the Board questioned the continuing viability of our N'port Factory. ^ I enc a copy of my own notes wh record the (main) viewpoints.

I shd like a full factual report, together w your assessment of the situation in time for our ~~Fri meeting~~ usual meeting on Fri (typist insert first Fri of next mth).

They have had a poor industrial relations record ^ (over the past 2 yrs) and we are coming under increaseding pressure fr Holstein Inc to increase efficiency.

bcc to Andrew Smyth.

Plse mark STRICTLY CONFIDENTIAL

Ref BH/KJ/141/yr initials

tabulated statement, move carriage/carrier to first tab stop and backspace one for each space between the columns **plus one**. At that point type last leader dot. Leave one space after the last typed character and then complete the leader dots.

5.6 If any item in the column takes more than one line, the leader dots should be typed only on the last line of the item.

5.7 When using grouped dots (5.2 for example) care must be taken to see that the groups of dots come underneath one another in all lines. To ensure this, you should adopt the following procedure: bring the carriage/carrier to the first tab stop set for the second column; backspace once for every space between first and second columns plus an extra two spaces. At this point set a tab stop. Backspace five from the tab stop just set, and set another tab stop. Continue in this way until you have reached the last word of the shortest line in the first column. Bring carriage/carrier back to margin and type first line, and using tab bar/key insert leader dots as and when required.

6 Subdivided column headings–centred style

Tabular statements may have subdivided columns. A column heading may be further divided into two or three separate items which are displayed beneath the main column heading as three separate columns. See the example below; the following explanatory steps, will give you an idea of how to proceed. Paper used is A5 landscape.

6.1 Set left and right margins and tab stops.

6.2 Centre and type main heading.

6.3 Type first horizontal line, turn up two single spaces.

6.4 Move carriage/carrier to tab stop 47(38), and tap in one space for every two characters and spaces in the longest items in the two columns beneath '9 nights', ie Twin Single, and half the number of spaces between the two columns. This will bring you to the centre point, ie 53(44). From this point backspace once for every two characters and spaces in the heading '9 nights'. At this point 49(40) type the heading. It will then be centred over the two columns beneath.

6.5 Move to tab stop 63(54), and tap in one space for every two characters and spaces in the longest items in the two columns beneath '12 nights', ie 1,025 Single, and half the number of spaces between the two columns. This will bring you to the centre point, ie 69(60). From this point backspace once for every two characters and spaces in the heading '12 nights'. At this point 65(56) type the heading. It will then be centred over the two columns beneath.

6.6 Turn up once and type the horizontal line. Mark the top of the vertical lines, and keep a note of the scale points. Turn up twice.

6.7 Type each of the words 'Twin' and 'Single' at the tab stops.

6.8 The two lines of the heading in the first column 'Departure on or between' must be centred vertically. The number of lines of typing and blank lines taken so far in typing the column headings is four. If the words 'Departure on' are typed on the line beneath '9 nights' '12 nights' and the words 'or between' typed on the line below that, they will be centred on the headings already typed.

6.9 With the alignment scale at the base of the words '9 nights', turn up one single space. From the left margin find the centre point of the longest line in the first column. From this point backspace once for every two letters and spaces in the line 'Departure on'. At scale point 27(18) type the words 'Departure on'. Turn up one single space.

6.10 Centre the next line 'or between' in the same way, and type it at scale point 28(19), then turn up two single spaces and type the horizontal line.

6.11 Turn up two single spaces and type the column items remembering to type units under units,

36(27) CRUISES – PRICES (PER PERSON)

21(12) ↓ ... ↓ 78(69)

27(18) Departure on or between	49(40) 9 nights		65(56) 12 nights	
	Twin	Single	Twin	Single
16 Oct 88	–	–	945	1,230
22 Oct 88 – 19 Nov 88	870	1,100	1,025	1,355

Left margin: 23(14)

Right margin: 79(70)
Tab stops:
47(38)
54(45)
63(54)
71(62)

Exercise 7

Type the following memo from Gay Hoyle to All Staff on A4 headed memo paper (see *Workguide and Resource Material*). Head your second page with the page number, today's date and All Staff on separate lines in double spacing.

(cc Frances Savage)

URGENT (top + 2 please)

(A CHARTERED) (please change Iraq to Dubai throughout)

NATIONAL RECRUITMENT CAMPAIGN – ENGINEERS

As you know, we have recently taken substantial advertising space in (insert 1) in an effort to ~~improve~~ induce a higher ~~level~~ no of ~~applications~~ applicants for current vacancies in Iraq. [We are now following up these adverts w a series of hospitality evenings in a no of locations. [(insert 2) [When discussing job opps w potential recruits it is important that y push

d ~~a~~ the early opps for exceptional candidates to take charge of substantial parts of the contract;

b highly-subsidized (catering) & quality air-conditioned accom, the tax-free salary, medical insurance (including on-site (dental) & (medical) facilities, 6 wks annual holiday, (end-of-contract bonus), & a gntee of suitable employment w the co on return to the UK;

a ~~&~~ our overseas welfare unit – indicating the high level of support given to ~~wives~~ wives, friends & families remaining in the UK; (or 1 of its associates)

c ~~d~~ the investment we have put into (the provision of) site facilities in Iraq – the sports & leisure ~~complex~~ club, the swimming pool, bars, European-style food, the book & video libraries, etc;

Nevertheless, to avoid unnecy repatriation costs you shd also mention

a the working wk (normally a ~~5~~ 6-day, ~~50~~ 60-hr wk before qualifying for overtime payment);

b the climatic conditions (top temperature to 30°C w a high degree of humidity);

d ~~&~~ ~~[struck-through line]~~;

c ~~&~~ (typist – take ~~(this item~~ Items C and D from the DataFiles, filename DUBAI, page 102.) (although Danish, Dutch, German & Swiss cos all operate in Iraq)

notches or round holes. Place the point of a pencil or suitable ball pen in one of these notches or holes and hold it in position against the paper with the right hand. With the left hand on the carriage release, you will obtain a continuous horizontal by running the carriage along. To avoid running the carriage too far, it is advisable to stop about two spaces before the scale point at which the horizontal line is to end, and then tap the space bar until the scale point is reached.

To make a vertical line, instead of running the carriage along, you release the cylinder ratchet by means of the interliner and turn the cylinder up with the left-hand knob. If the vertical lines extend almost to the bottom of the page, it is better to rule these by hand after the paper has been removed from the machine, to avoid the paper slipping when the cylinder is turned down for the start of the next line. After you have had some practice in ruling in this way, you will find that it saves a great deal of time, particularly if carbon copies are being taken. On your electronic typewriter there may be a function key for inserting vertical lines.

3.9 If you wish to make a very clear distinction between sections of a table, the horizontal and vertical lines can be emphasized by double or thicker ruled lines. With electronic keyboards, the **bold** function key may be used.

4 *Multiple-line headings*

Where column headings consist of more than one line or are of unequal depth, they are always typed in single spacing. They are never underscored in a **ruled** table.

4.1 **Blocked style**

- 4.1.1 Set margins and tab stops.
- 4.1.2 All column headings start on the second single space after the main or subheading. However, if the table is ruled, then the column headings will start on the second single space after the first horizontal line.
- 4.1.3 The heading over the first column is typed at the left margin.
- 4.1.4 Headings in other columns start at the tab stop set for the beginning of the longest line in the column. Each line in any one heading will start at the same scale point. The £ sign is usually typed above the first figure of the £'s.

4.2 **Centred style**

Each line of a column heading is centred horizontally within the space allocated for the longest line in that column/heading. The whole of the heading in any one column is centred vertically in the space allocated for the deepest heading.

When typing multiple-line headings, proceed as follows:

- 4.2.1 Turn up two single spaces after the main/subheading or, if a ruled table, turn up two single spaces after the first horizontal line.
- 4.2.2 Type the deepest heading first.
- 4.2.3 Move carriage/carrier to tab stop set for column with deepest heading.
- 4.2.4 If the longest line is the column itself, then all lines in the column heading are centred on the longest line in the column.
- 4.2.5 If the longest line is the column heading, then that line is typed at the tab stop and all other lines in the heading centred on it.
- 4.2.6 Find the centre point by tapping once for each two spaces/characters in the longest line. Make a note of this point.
- 4.2.7 Backspace one for each two characters/spaces in the line to be centred. Type the line at the point reached.
- 4.2.8 In this way centre and type all lines in the heading.
- 4.2.9 Move to the next deepest heading.
- 4.2.10 Count the number of lines in this heading and subtract the number from the number of lines in the deepest heading just typed. Divide the result by two; eg:

Deepest heading	5 lines
Next deepest	2
Difference	3
Divide by two	1½—turn up one and a half spaces from first line of deepest heading.

- 4.2.11 Turn the cylinder towards you so that the alignment scale is at the base of the first line of the deepest heading just typed. From this point turn up one and a half spaces and start typing the next deepest heading. Use the same method as in 4.2.6 and 4.2.7.
- 4.2.12 Continue with other column headings in the same way.

5 *Leader dots (leader lines)*

Leader dots (full stops) are used to guide the eye along lines from one column to another. There are four methods of grouping which may be used, viz:

5.1 One dot three spaces . . . .

5.2 Two dots three spaces . .   . .

5.3 Three dots two spaces . . . .

5.4 Continuous dots . . . .

5.5 Continuous dots are the simplest and are recommended unless you receive instructions to the contrary. Type leader dots lightly and evenly. When using continuous leader dots in a

All candidates are given a medical (exam) at the [in full] [time of] formal interview. [Working in Iraq is not the ~~f~~ [F]oreign Legion! We hve prepared a video (Insert 3). Contracts are currently for ~~3~~ [2] or ~~$~~ [3] yrs.

Wd Frances please ensure th suff quantities of our 'Working Overseas w Us' info packs are available at all functions.

Circulation: Mike Bradford
George Rose
Tim Barton
Barry Decker
Barry Savage } Swindon office
Vic Sturgess Runcorn "
Dave Miller Blackheath "

Ref GH/0110

(1) The Daily Telegraph, Civil Engineer & Engineering Weekly.

3 (~~2~~) wh shows the working environment & records interviews w expatriates.

2 (~~3~~) For this contract we are particularly looking for [fully-qualified civil] engineers under ~~the~~ 35 yrs of age, who have had some yrs' exp of motorway & bridge construction, including beam placing, & who are capable of managing a keen but unskilled workforce.

We always prefer applicants who can offer previous exp of ~~overseas contracts~~ work in any capacity.

The Iraqi authorities have brought in large nos of Asian construction workers, many of whom need further guidance & training to bring there work up to the required standard columns. Set tab stop at point reached for start of third column.

1.11 Continue in the same way for any additional columns.

NOTES: (a) If **blocked** style is being used, follow items 1.6–1.11 and type main heading at left margin.

(b) The number of spaces left between columns depends on the total width of the table. A minimum of three and a maximum of seven are recommended.

2 Column headings

2.1 **Blocked** Set margins and tab stops. Turn up two single spaces after the main/subheading or, if a ruled table, turn up two single spaces after the first horizontal line. The heading over the first column is typed at the left margin. Headings in the other columns start at the tab stop set for the beginning of the longest line of each column (could be heading or column item). The £ sign is usually typed above the first figure of the £'s.

The column **items** are typed at the tab stops set for the start of the longest item. With figures, remember to type units under units and tens under tens, etc.

2.2 **Centred** Set margins and tab stops. If the **column heading** is **longer** than the column items and if there is only one line in the heading, type it at the left margin or at the tab stop set. If there is more than one line in a column heading, see instructions under **multiple-line** column headings.

Before typing the **column items**, clear tab stop already set, find centre point of column by tapping space bar once for every two characters and spaces in the heading (this will give you the centre point of the heading) then backspace one for every two characters and spaces in the longest column item. Set a tab stop at point reached. If the column items are words, this scale point will give you the starting point for each item in the column. If the column items are figures, units must be typed under units and tens under tens.

Where the **column heading** is **shorter** than the **longest item** in the column, find the centre point of the longest column item by tapping space bar once for every two characters and spaces in that item. From the point reached, backspace once for every two characters and spaces in the heading. At this point type the heading. If there is more than one line in a column heading, see instructions under **multiple-line** headings.

3 Ruling

Tabulated statements are sometimes made more effective and clearer by ruling horizontal and/or vertical lines. Although it is assumed that you have already learnt how to rule up tabulated work, the following notes will serve as a reminder.

3.1 If horizontal lines only are ruled, use the underscore and let the lines project two spaces beyond the margins on either side.

3.2 Always turn up one single space before a horizontal underscore and two single spaces after.

3.3 If both horizontal and vertical lines are required, rule these (a) either by underscore, in which case the paper has to be removed from the machine after the table has been typed, and reinserted sideways for the ruling of the vertical lines; or (b) by ink; or (c) a combination of the two, eg horizontals by underscore, verticals by ink. See that the ink ruling is the same colour as the underscore line.

3.4 The vertical lines between the columns must be ruled exactly in the middle of each blank space. It is therefore advisable to leave an odd number of spaces between the columns—one for the vertical ruling and an equal number on either side of the ruling. The points on the scale at which the vertical lines are to be ruled should be marked by light pencil marks at the top **and** bottom of the columns.

3.5 To find the point at which to mark the vertical line, proceed as follows: (It is assumed that you have left either three, five or seven spaces between columns.) (a) Move to tab stop following first vertical line. (b) If you have left three spaces between columns, backspace two and make a pencil mark; if you have left five spaces between, backspace three; if seven spaces between, backspace four.

3.6 Move to second and other columns and repeat 3.5.

NOTE: Do not extend the vertical lines above or below the horizontals—see that they meet precisely.

3.7 **Ink** If horizontal and vertical lines are to be ruled in ink, follow the same procedures as for ruling by underscore, but in this case the beginning and end of each horizontal line must be marked in pencil, as well as the vertical lines. When the table has been completed, remove paper from machine and, with a fine nib, rule lines carefully and neatly to scale points marked. It is essential that vertical and horizontal lines meet exactly.

3.8 **Typewriter** Apart from the use of the underscore, on most modern typewriters provision is made for the speedy ruling of both horizontal and vertical lines. On the alignment scale/card holder you will find two small

COMPOSING CORRESPONDENCE FROM BRIEF NOTES

Exercise 1

Compose a memo from Diane Harrod, Customer Relations to Alan Gerrard in Marketing.

Use a subject heading of Monthly Planning Meeting. Say that, unfortunately, I shall not be able to make his planning meeting next Tuesday (*give date*) as I have been called to an urgent meeting in London. I will ring him on my return on Thursday (*include next Thursday's date*) to discuss advertising budgets for the new product lines.

Exercise 2

Compose a memo from Mike Ashworth, Production Manager to Gail Pinter in Personnel.

Use a subject heading of Engineering Recruitment. Say that I should like to know what response she had to our advertisement in last month's *Engineering Monthly* for draughtsmen. I am free to shortlist applications on either Tuesday or Wednesday next week (*give dates*) and suggest formal interviewing takes place early next month. Perhaps she can telephone me on Thursday or Friday?

Exercise 3

Letter from Brian Shelley to Dr Jorgen Bergen (*address from Data files, filename Alpha, page 102*).

Thank Dr Bergen for his letters of 13 Oct and 16 Jan and apologize for not having replied before. Say that we have been having lots of meetings recently about the planning of our new stand and that many of his suggestions have been put forward to the planning committee. As a result, we have built a number of his ideas into this year's programme. Express our sincere thanks for taking the trouble to give us the benefit of his ideas.

Exercise 4

Letter from Lynne Eastmann to Mark Phelps (*address from Data files, filename Alpha, page 102*).

Thank Mark for his excellent contribution to last quarter's *Management Education* journal—enclose a number of copies for his personal use. We would like him to provide us with a short article (about 2,000 words) on the Chartered Management Initiative for inclusion in our autumn newsletter. We will need the final copy by the end of next month. We are able to pay him a fee of £80 plus any research expenses he may incur. Can he let us know whether he is prepared to do this by the end of the month?

You should be able to compose your correspondence direct on to your screen and then use 'cut and paste' functions to edit it.

Sums of money in columns

See ***Totals***, page 152.

Sums of money in context

1 If the sum comprises only pounds, type as follows: £5, £10 or £5.00, £10.00.
2 If only pence, type: 10p, 7p.

NOTE: **No** space between figures and letter p, and no full stop after p (unless, of course, it ends a sentence).

3 With mixed amounts, ie sums comprising pounds and pence, the decimal point and the £ symbol should always be used, but **not** the abbreviation p.

Example
£70.05. The £ sign and p should **never** appear together.

4 If the sum contains a decimal point but no whole pounds, a nought should be typed after the £ symbol and before the point. Example: £0.97.

5 Thousands may be represented by a capital K, eg £20,000 = £20K.

Superscripts—superior (raised) characters

Some characters have to be typed above the normal typing line, such as degrees (small o), mathematical formulae and raised reference marks. These are called superscripts.

1 If your typewriter has half linespacing, proceed as follows:
  1.1 Turn cylinder back half a space.
  1.2 Type superscript(s).
  1.3 Return cylinder to original typing line.
2 If your typewriter does not have half spacing, proceed as follows:
  2.1 Release from linespacing mechanism by means of the interliner lever.
  2.2 Turn cylinder back about half a linespace.
  2.3 Type superscript(s).
  2.4 Return interliner to normal position.
  2.5 See that cylinder returns to original typing line.

Tabulation

There are many kinds of statements and records that the typist may have to set out in tabulated form.

As you gain experience in the different forms of display, you should be able to look at a script and decide what margins are suitable. With tabulation, it is often possible to study a table and decide on a left margin. In other cases, all that will be necessary is to type out the longest line in each column, or tap out the longest line of each column (together with the spaces between columns) and see whether the table will fit in with the margins already set (within a document you are already typing) or whether a 25 mm (1 inch) left margin would be adequate.

In other situations, it will give a better result if you use the backspacing method for the horizontal centring and adopt the following procedure:

1 Main headings and columns without headings

1.1 Clear margin stops and all previous tab stops.
1.2 Insert paper with left edge at 0.
1.3 Calculate number of vertical lines in exercise and subtract this number from number of vertical lines on paper being used. Divide answer by two and add one to this figure: turn up this number from top edge of paper. Example using A5 landscape paper:

Number of vertical lines in A5 landscape paper	35	
Less number of lines in exercise to be typed, say	22	
Divide by two	13 ÷ 2 = 6	(ignore
Plus one	1	fractions)
Turn up	7	

1.4 Bring carriage to horizontal centre point of paper.
1.5 If **centred** style is being used, from centre point of paper backspace once for every two characters and spaces in the main heading and type heading at point reached. Turn up two single spaces.
1.6 Mark the longest line in each column. From the centre of the paper backspace once for every two characters and spaces in the longest line of each column, carrying any odd letter to the next column.
1.7 Backspace once for every two spaces to be left between the columns, including any odd number left over in step 1.6.
1.8 Set margin stop at point reached.
1.9 From left margin, tap space bar once for each letter and space in the longest line of the first column, and once for each blank space between the first and second columns. Set tab stop at point reached for start of second column.
1.10 From the first tab stop, again tap space bar once for each character and space in the longest item of the second column, and once for each blank space between second and third

SKILL BUILDING 2

1 *Alphabetic sentences*

Type each sentence twice.

We enjoyed the visits to the London theatres and frequently seized the opportunity to do some shopping in Oxford Street before going back.

The brand new magazine which looks at fashion and beauty is very enjoyable and quite exceptional value.

2 *Improve control of words using all fingers*

appointments photographics representation placings applications pleasing

publications spherical stipulate superficial desperation speculation

3 *Improve control of words with common prefixes*

considerable continue contact consultant contract control conversation

computer complex combination company comparison competition compulsory

interior intermediate international internal interruption interview

undercut understand undertake underwrite underground underhand underlie

transport transcription transfer transaction translation transmission

4 *Production development from manuscript*

Reading time: 1 minute   Target typing time: 2 minutes

The Northern Hotel Group announces the launch of it's management dev'ment courses for women.

Broadly the course covers dealing w superiors, colleagues, subordinates, assertiveness &, negotiating skills, and provides a personnel dev'ment plan. There are ~~25~~ 30 free places. To apply you shd enclose a (CV), provide a sep statement (of no more than 300 words) explaining why you need this course and send it to us immed. The course runs from 4–12 Aug.

(type out in full)

500 keystrokes (100 words)

Specialized typing

Technical and legal work—specifications, articles of agreement, wills, plays, etc—are specialized documents and layout often varies from one office to another.

Management will supply the typist with copies of previous documents and these should be followed precisely. In offices today, the skeleton forms of much of this specialized work are held on disks and the typist can locate quite easily any one particular document on the disk, type in the information applicable to a client, and then have the document automatically typed out.

One or two examples of these documents are given in this book. Follow the layout or instructions given.

Speeches

The amount of time spent on preparing and typing a speech will depend on a number of factors such as:

1 The degree of formality.
2 The nature of the topic.
3 The speaker's knowledge of the topic.
4 The length of the speech.
5 The amount of research necessary to verify data such as names, dates, historic facts, statistics, quotations, etc.
6 Whether a copy, or summary, is required as a press release.
7 Whether the speaker requires:
  7.1 Notes—essential points only (usually typed on postcards).
  7.2 Quotations and statistics only.
  7.3 The speech typed in full.

If the speech will be read verbatim, use pica typeface (or a larger typeface if you have one available) and double/treble spacing. No doubt the speaker will tell you what points, or headings, he wishes to emphasize and upper case/emboldening/underlining (preferably in red), should be employed to highlight these objectives.

Perhaps the speaker may have a number of asides, jokes, quotations, etc, that she/he may, or may not, use, and it would be preferable to type these separately so that they may be utilized as and when appropriate or, perhaps, not at all, depending on the audience and their reactions.

Some speakers are very particular about using notations for 'stage directions', pauses, jesticulations, etc, and, where this is the case, leave wide side margins for reminders. In addition, speakers often wish to enhance their speech by audio-visual materials, overhead transparencies, etc, and the point of presentation should be indicated in the margin(s).

When typing a speech in full, the suggestions given for ***Reports***, page 139, will be helpful.

Spelling

See ***Deliberate errors***, page 116 and ***Abbreviations***, page 104.

Square brackets

See ***Special signs, symbols and marks***, page 143.

Standard margins

NOTE: In business, and in most examinations, you will have to decide on the margin settings: therefore, in many exercises we will not give you margins either in 12 or 10 pitch. Use the following short table as a guide.

Paper	*Typing line*	*12 pitch*	*10 pitch*
A5 portrait	50 spaces	13–63	6–56
A4 and A5 landscape	60 spaces	22–82	12–72
	70 spaces	18–88	6–76*
	80 spaces	13–93	not suitable
Memoranda		13–90	11–75

* Use only in exceptional circumstances

Standard paragraphs

Many organizations assemble a file of standard paragraphs covering routine replies to enquiries. The originator then indicates on the enquiry letter the numbers, or codes, of the standard paragraphs to be typed in reply, together with variable information where necessary. The typist copies the paragraphs in the sequence indicated by the originator; thus no time is needed for creative composition or dictation. With certain electronic typewriters, and word processors, the standard paragraphs are coded and stored, then retrieved and automatically inserted as and where required.

See also ***Forms (Automation)***, page 124.

Subscripts—inferior (lowered) characters

Subscripts are characters that have to be typed below the normal typing line as in chemical formulae.

1 If your typewriter has half linespacing, proceed as follows:
  1.1 Turn cylinder forward (away from you) half a space.
  1.2 Type subscript(s).
  1.3 Return cylinder to original typing line.
2 If your typewriter does not have half spacing, proceed as follows:
  2.1 Release cylinder from linespacing mechanism by means of the interliner lever.
  2.2 Turn cylinder forward about half a linespace.
  2.3 Type subscript(s).
  2.4 Return interliner to normal position.
  2.5 See that cylinder returns to original typing line.

Exercise 1

Type the following address labels using the pre-printed sheet from the *Workguide and Resource Material*. Type the post town and the country in capitals in all cases and omit all accents on capital letters. For details of how to type overseas addresses see page 111.

M Paul Janssen, NV Prodata SA, Avenue de Tervurenlaan 419, Bruxelles 1150, Belgium

H Hans Wergner, Spectra GmbH, Siemensstrasse 80, D-6100 Darmstadt, ~~The Netherlands~~ West Germany

John Gale Esq, 110 The Rampart, Castlecraig 2051, Australia — mark AIRMAIL

M Jacques Carella, ~~Systems Analyst~~, 94 Avenue Hoche, 75771 Paris, France

H Franz Frei, Koordination Informatik, Limmastrasse 442, Postfach 266, CH-8031 Zürich, Switzerland

H Sven Eric Gustavsson, Errpege I Gävle AB, Engelbrektsgatan 2, S.803 54 Gävle, Sweden

H = Herrn M = Monsieur - please type in full

Exercise 2

Type the following advertisement on plain A5 paper. Retain K (K = 1,000).

Media Premiere

For the Top Jobs in Media } centre and emphasize headings

Travel Editor London c £22K

Advertising (Kent) up to £40K

Graphic Designer (Oxon) c £18K

Researcher Norwich £12K-£15K

~~Technical Advisor~~ Copywriter London £19K

News ~~Editor~~ Reporter (West Mid) £neg

Local Radio (Merseyside) £15K

A/c Manager London £25K-£30K } OTE

Current Affairs Producer (London) £neg

Economics Editor Paris £35K

Interested in any of the above

Ring us, or write (enclosing a cv): } centre

Mike Howard or ~~Daljit Sechra~~ Fabienne de Laet, Media Premiere (add address and telephone no from Data Files, Alpha, page 102)

~~(0734)~~ (24-hr recorded answering service)

Special signs, symbols and marks

A variety of words (sign, symbol, mark) is used when referring to the characters on this page. One speaks of punctuation marks, the brace symbol and the £ sign. The word symbol is employed mainly for mathematical and scientific formulae and in computer terminology.

Degree	Small o, raised half a space.	6°
Feet	Apostrophe typed after the figure(s).	8'
Inches	Double quotation marks typed immediately after figure(s).	7"
Minus	To show subtraction—hyphen with space either side.	6 - 4 = 2
Minutes	Apostrophe typed immediately after figure(s).	10'
Multiplication	Small x with a space either side.	4 x 5
Seconds	Double quotation marks typed immediately after figure(s).	9"
To	Hyphen or dash.	21-25

Constructing special signs, symbols and marks

Some characters, not provided on the keyboard, can be typed by combining two characters, ie by typing one character, backspacing and then typing the second character, or by typing one character and then the second immediately afterwards. In a few cases the interliner must be used to allow the characters to be raised or lowered.

Asterisk	Small x and hyphen.	x̶
Brace	Continuous brackets typed one underneath the other.	( ) ( ) ( )
Caret	Underscore and oblique.	∠
Cedilla	Small c and comma.	ç
Cent	Small or capital C and oblique.	¢ C/
Dagger	Capital I and hyphen.	†
Diaeresis	Quotation marks.	ü
Divide into	Right bracket and underscore on line above.	)‾‾‾‾
Division	Hyphen, backspace and type colon.	÷
Dollar	Capital S, backspace and type oblique.	$
Double dagger	Capital I raised half a space, backspace and type another capital I slightly below; or capital I and equation sign.	‡
Equation	Two hyphens—one slightly above the other.	=
Exclamation	Apostrophe, backspace and type full stop.	!
Paragraph	Small c and lowered capital I.	¶
Plus	Hyphen and lowered apostrophe.	+
Section	Two capital S's or two small s's.	§ §
Square brackets	Oblique and underscore.	[ ]
Square root	Small v and oblique, followed by underscore on line above.	√‾‾‾
Thousand	Capital K.	£20,000 = £20K
Umlaut	Quotation marks.	ü

On modern typewriters many of the above characters are provided. On others, it is difficult to type the division or plus as combined characters. Where this is the case, it would be wise to insert these in matching-colour ink.

When the **asterisk** has to be typed in the body of the text, it is typed as a superscript (raised character). Before typing the combination asterisk, turn the cylinder one half space towards you, type small x, backspace and type hyphen; then turn back to normal typing line. Where the asterisk is already fitted, **do not** lower the paper before typing, as the sign on the typeface is already raised.

To type a **square bracket** take the following steps:

Left bracket

1 Type oblique sign.
2 Backspace one and type underscore.
3 Turn cylinder back one full linespace and type underscore.
4 Turn cylinder up one full linespace, backspace once and continue with typing up to the right bracket.

Right bracket

1 Type oblique sign.
2 Backspace two and type underscore.
3 Turn cylinder back one full linespace and type underscore.
4 Turn cylinder up one single space, tap space bar once and continue typing.

Exercise 3

Display the following advertisement on a postcard.

Help People Stop Smoking.... — Emphasize heading

We are organizing a one-day programme ~~of~~ helping people to stop smoking. The programme includes factual info on the detrimental effects of smoking on health, advice on setting up support groups, practical aspects of helping smoking people to stop, & guidance to help people remain non-smokers.

[~~taking a~~ covering a number of aspects]

Tel (0503) 445501 (x 221)

Exercise 4

Type the following menu on A5 paper.

```
***    *    *    *    *    *    *    ***
  Lincolnshire Chamber of Commerce   } Centre & emphasize
  Anniversary Luncheon               } each line *
*       Menu
              or
  Potage Crème d'~~Asperges~~
*  Salade aux Crevettes                 *
       *   *   *                  [Use asterisks to sep courses throughout]
*  Sole à la Dieppoise                  *
       *   *   *
   Gigot ~~à Farci~~, ~~en croûte~~ Bedouin
*  Poularde à la Albuféra               *
   Selection of Veg                  [type border as indicated]
*      *   *   *                        *
   Pêches ~~Surprise~~ ~~Cardinal~~
*  Crêpes Suzette                       *
       *   *   *
   Coffee & Mints
*                                       *
   [the info about wine will be found in the
*  DataFiles - Filename menu, page 103]  *
***    *    *    *    *    *    *    ***
```

Key in exercise 4 (filename MENU) for 12-pitch printout. Use the automatic centring function to centre each line and the automatic underline function for the first heading. When you have completed this task, save under filename MENU. Recall the document and follow the instructions for text editing on page 100.

4 *Fitting a new ribbon*

The manufacturer always supplies a handbook with a new typewriter and complete instructions will be given on how to change the ribbon. Before removing the old ribbon, look very carefully at how it is threaded. Then:

4.1 Wind the old ribbon on to one spool and detach the end, noting how it is hooked to the spool.
4.2 Discard old spool and ribbon.
4.3 Fasten end of the new ribbon on to the empty spool.
4.4 Depress shift lock; this makes it easier to thread the ribbon into the carrier.
4.5 Place both spools in their sockets.
4.6 Thread ribbon through carrier.
4.7 **Cartridge ribbon** This ribbon is enclosed in a cartridge which clips on to spindles, and it is not necessary to handle the ribbon when threading it through the ribbon guides.

Roman numerals

1 Units I (1) X (10) C (100) M (1000)
Fives V (5) L (50) D (500)

2 The four *unit* symbols can be repeated to express two or three units of the *same* symbol.

Examples

1 = I	2 = II	3 = III
10 = X	20 = XX	30 = XXX
100 = C	200 = CC	300 = CCC
1000 = M	2000 = MM	3000 = MMM

3 The symbol I may be used or repeated (up to III) *after* any of the above units or fives, in which case it *adds* to the symbol in front.

Examples

I = 1	VI = 6	XI = 11	LI = 51
II = 2	VII = 7	XII = 12	LII = 52
III = 3	VIII = 8	XIII = 13	LIII = 53

CI = 101	DI = 501	MI = 1001
CII = 102	DII = 502	MII = 1002
CIII = 103	DIII = 503	MIII = 1003

4 To express 4, 9, 40, 400 and 900, take the symbol immediately *above* and put the appropriate unit symbol *in front*, which means that *it is subtracted* from the higher symbol.

4 = *5* − 1 = IV
40 = *50* − 10 = XL
400 = *500* − 100 = CD
9 = *10* − 1 = IX
90 = *100* − 10 = XC
900 = *1000* − 100 = CM.

NOTE: I can be placed *only* before V or X;
X can be placed *only* before L or C;
C can be placed *only* before D or M.

5 To express numbers other than those in point 4, take the unit of five symbol immediately *below* and *add* to it the remaining symbols by putting these *after* the unit or five symbol.

Examples
6 = *5* + 1 = VI
7 = *5* + 2 = VII
8 = *5* + 3 = VIII
14 = *10* + 4 = XIV
15 = *10* + 5 = XV
16 = *10* + 6 = XVI
17 = *10* + 7 = XVII
18 = *10* + 8 = XVIII

60 = *50* + 10 = LX
70 = *50* + 20 = LXX
80 = *50* + 30 = LXXX
600 = *500* + 100 = DC
700 = *500* + 200 = DCC
800 = *500* + 300 = DCCC

6 A horizontal line drawn over the unit symbol means that the unit is multiplied by 1000.

Example
$\bar{M}$ = 1000 × 1000 = 1,000,000.

7 To convert arabic figures into roman numerals, take each figure in turn.

Example
To convert 467, proceed as follows:
400 = 500 − 100 = CD; 60 = 50 + 10 = LX;
7 = 5 + 2 = VII; 467 = CDLXVII.

8 Used as follows:
For monarchs, form and class numbers, chapters, preface pages, tables or paragraphs. Sometimes to express the year, enumerations, subsections, etc.

Single-element typewriters

There are now many electric/electronic typewriters with single-element heads. These typewriters have no movable carriage, which also means that the cylinder is static, and there are no type bars. Instead, they have a printing head attached to a carrier that moves across the page from left to right, stroke by stroke. When you wish to return the carrier to the left margin, you press the return key as you would with the ordinary electric typewriter.

The printing element may be a golf ball head which whirls and tilts to make an impression on the paper, or it may be a daisywheel which is a rapidly spinning disk of flexible arms, and on the tip of each arm there is a typeface character. The required character stops at the printing point and is struck by a small hammer which impinges the image on the paper.

See also ***Electronic typewriters***, page 117.

Exercise 5

Type this advertisement in single spacing, centring each line and following the suggested line-endings. Rule as shown.

One airline
has more flights
to SA than
the total no from all
the other airlines put together.

We bel that if its yr
bus to be in any part
of SA then
its our bus
to take you.

(type South America in full)

(leave a line blank)

Set a centred tab stop to type this exercise.

Exercise 6

Type this advertisement, following the line-endings as indicated. Align the right margin so that the finished work is triangular in shape.

(Please rule round the triangle when you have finished.)

(type Hong Kong in full)

You
wake to
encounter the
true magnificence
of HK harbour,
& sip our freshly-brewed
morning coffee before partaking
of ~~a~~ an [sumptuous] English, or authentic
HK-style breakfast. You are now
able to face the bustle of the world outside.

(leave a blank line)

You return, tired & spent, at the end of yr
[gruelling] bus day to warmth, elegance [& a luxurious standard of service wh few hotels can provide. We are [after all] one of ~~the~~]
the Worlds finest
international
hotels
. . .

When a stencil is to be cut, the following points should be noted:

1 Thoroughly clean the typefaces so that no character is clogged. With elite type brush the typeface frequently during the cutting of the stencil.
2 Carbon paper is supplied with the stencils; the object of this is twofold: in the first place it helps to avoid the chipping out of certain characters, and, secondly, it makes the stencil easier to read for checking purposes.
3 Place a sheet of this carbon paper, coated side upwards, between the stencil and the backing sheet which is attached to the stencil. Also, place another sheet of carbon paper with the coated side towards the backing sheet. This will give a carbon copy on the backing sheet and will simplify checking.
4 When you insert the stencil into the typewriter, see that the line or scale at the top of the stencil is level with the alignment scale. If necessary, adjust it in the ordinary way by means of the paper release lever. The figures shown down each side of the stencil correspond with the vertical linespacing of the typewriter. The horizontal numbers represent pica and elite letter-spacing.
5 Note the frame of the stencil, and be careful not to type outside this.*
6 A firm, sharp and even touch is required for striking the keys, but certain letters need to be struck more heavily than others: letters such as m, w, and particularly, upper-case letters. More open letters, such as o, c, e, underscore and punctuation marks, need a lighter stroke, as otherwise the centres may fall out. If this does happen, type the letter on a piece of spare stencil, and with a pin and speck of correction fluid insert the letter in the space.
7 After the stencil has been typed, check it carefully before you take it out of the machine.
8 Although you should avoid making mistakes, an error can be rectified by the use of correction fluid. The procedure is as follows:
   8.1 Turn the cylinder up a few lines.
   8.2 Flatten the letters to be corrected.
   8.3 Put a pencil or flat ruler underneath the stencil (just above or below the word to be corrected) so as to separate it from the carbon.
   8.4 Paint out the error with a very small quantity of correction fluid. Leave for a few seconds to dry, then remove pencil or ruler, and type the correct letter(s) or word(s).**

* It is advisable to leave at least 13 mm ($\frac{1}{2}$ inch) clear space (inside the frame) at the top and sides of the stencil.

** If the fluid in the bottle has become thick, it should not be used.

9 By holding up the finished stencil to the light, you will be able to see if there are any characters either 'overcut' or 'undercut', and this will enable you to adjust your touch for future stencils.

NOTE: Special stencils are available for use with the daisywheel.

Reverse side of paper (typing on)

If the continuation sheet is typed on the reverse side of the paper, the margins are also reversed, eg if the first page was typed with margins of elite 19–88, pica 11–76, typing on the reverse side would be with margins of 13–83 and 6–73.

If you use equal left and right margins, this will save altering the settings when using the reverse side.

Ribbons (typewriter)

1 Fabric ribbons

Fabric ribbons are made of silk, nylon or cotton and may be monochrome (one colour—usually black) or bichrome (two colours—the top half black and the bottom half red). Bichrome ribbons are not economical, unless the red is used frequently. You can type on the bottom half of the ribbon by putting the ribbon switch on 'red'.

2 Film ribbons

The more expensive the ribbon the better the finished product will look and the easier it will be to make a correction.

Single-strike correctable carbon film ribbon can be used once only, but it gives a top-quality finish. Excellent for typing offset-litho masters.

Multi-strike film ribbon can be used once only, but it lasts approximately four times longer than the single-strike ribbon because the points at which the characters strike the ribbon overlap each other. The appearance of the typescript is not so perfect as that produced by the single-strike carbon film ribbon.

3 Correction ribbons

A correction ribbon is used for correcting typing errors. It may be the bottom half of the carbon ribbon or it may be completely separate on additional spools. To correct a typing error, switch to the correction ribbon, type the same error (the correction ribbon will 'lift' the impression from the paper). Switch to normal ribbon and type correct letter(s).

Exercise 7

Rule a sheet of A4 landscape paper into three equal portions. Display the following on each portion, as indicated.

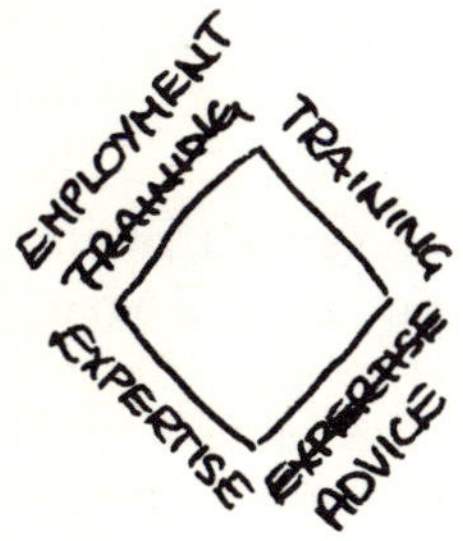

EMPLOYMENT LEGISLATION
ARE YOU UP TO DATE?

JOINTLY SPONSORED BY:
NEXX ADVISORY SERVICES
LKP CORPORATION, USA

(FIRST PORTION)

WHAT WL IT COVER?

To begin
- job descriptions/specifications
- using advertising agencies
- forms standardization
- legal aspects of interviewing

Forming the Contract
- offer & acceptance
- consideration
- (illegality)
- (mistake & misrepresentation)

Contract Terms
- written particulars
- contract & custom
- implied terms
- statutory minimum protection

Discrimination
- sex ↑ & marital status
- (race)
- disabled
- children & young persons
- foreign subjects

(SECOND PORTION)

WORKSHOP LEADERS ↕ leave 1" here

JANET DAVISON MIPM & PHILIP NEWELL
FIPM are principles of NEXX
Adv Ser - a consultancy special-
izing in personnel/employment law
& (IR).
Janet has become ack'd for her
ability to present complex info
in a readily understandable form.
[Philip has had considerable exp
in the representation of both
respondents & applicants at
Industrial Tribunals ~~and~~
~~Employment Appeal Tribunals~~.
He assists many cos in ~~developing~~
the dev'ment of ~~new~~ recruitment
policies and procedures.
FEES
£155 + £23.25 VAT (including
morning coffee, lunch & after-
noon tea. It does not include
accom or drinks.
PAYMENT SHD BE MADE
BEFORE THE EVENT

(THIRD PORTION)

double or treble spacing with wide margins—38 mm × 25 mm (1½ inches × 1 inch). The final typing should be single spacing with appropriate spacing between headings, paragraphs, etc.

Quotations

When preparing a business report, an executive may wish to quote excerpts from other sources. Brief quotations run in with text matter that introduces them. These are enclosed in quotation marks. Longer quotations, say more than four lines, should be started on a new line and preferably indented from the left margin (or both margins). Quotation marks are put at the beginning of each paragraph and at the **end** of the last paragraph. Permission to use a quotation should be requested from the copyright owner.

Reprography

Offset process

Many printers now use a process called offset duplicating to reproduce material. This process is also known as offset-litho (lithography) and, in recent years, has become very popular. The business printing department often combines a word processing department with a reprographics centre where material that has been prepared on word processors is duplicated.

Various types of masters are available for offset duplicating. Some are plastic, some are metal, and others are made of special photographic paper and are produced by a photographic process.

The direct-image master consists of a sheet of plasticized paper on which you type, draw or write. Any drawing or handwriting must be done with special offset supplies. The direct-image master usually has preprinted guidelines at the top and sides.

It should be noted that to get satisfactory results from an offset master, you need a carbon film ribbon. Another essential for good results in offset is that the master should be kept as clean as possible. Fingerprints, smudges and bends result in ink blobs in those same shapes on the finished copies.

Errors are easily corrected with a special offset eraser or with correction fluid. You simply erase the incorrect letter(s) lightly with this eraser, taking care not to damage the master. If you erase too heavily, you will break the surface of the master and a dark mark will appear on the duplicated copies. Use the correction fluid with great care. If you apply too much, a dark patch will appear on all the duplicated copies.

Most typists type an original on plain paper and then have this photographed on to an offset master. When correcting errors on this original, use correction fluid not an eraser.

Photocopying

Because of their versatility and speed, photocopiers are now replacing duplicators. They can reduce or enlarge copy, and the more sophisticated models have collating facilities which enable lengthy documents to be photocopied and the pages automatically collated and stapled; also, some photocopiers will print in colour.

It is now fairly common practice to use the photocopier instead of taking a carbon copy(ies) or in place of taking extra originals through the word processor or electronic typewriter. When sending out a business letter to a customer, always send the original.

Photocopiers cost money—time, maintenance, electricity, better-quality paper and other supplies—therefore, only make copies that are absolutely necessary and do not 'run off' a few more just in case they might be needed!

If you are typing an original only on a manual or electric typewriter, then not taking a carbon copy does save time as any corrections are more easily made.

Stencil process

By this process a master copy or stencil is prepared, the required matter being typed on a stencil sheet which is made of special wax-like paper. When the stencil has been prepared, it is attached to a drum on a rotary machine, of which there are many different makes, but all of these work on more or less the same principle. The paper used for the copies is called duplicating paper and is fed through the rotary duplicator, pressed against the drum, and ink is forced through the cut-out forms of the characters.

When a stencil is 'cut' by typewriter, the ribbon is switched out of action, so that the typeface strikes on to the stencil without passing through the ribbon, thus producing a clear-cut character. Special stylus pens can also be obtained for drawing lines or for handwriting.

Colour work can be produced on rotary duplicators. This entails having a different drum for each colour, but the drum containing the ink can be changed in a few seconds. In this case, however, a separate stencil must be prepared for each colour instead of the whole of the matter being typed on one stencil, and this necessitates care being taken to see that each colour comes precisely in the required position on the completed document.

Exercise 8

The following four-page leaflet should be typed on A4 paper (both sides). Display as attractively as you can.

FRONT COVER — centre each word on a sep line in spaced caps

New 'Freeway' Superstore in Enfield

Opening times from 1 Sept:

Mon ..	..	..	..	9.00 am to	7.00 pm
Tue ..	..	..	..	"	"
Wed ..	..	..	..	"	"
Thurs	..	..	..	"	9
Fri ..	..	..	..	"	"
Sat ..	..	..	..	8.30	7

INSIDE FRONT

Easy Payment: cash dispensers for all the major banks, free cheque cashing, credit cards accepted

More convenience: 30 modern checkouts, (insert 1) free carrier bags, toilets (with disabled facilities), free play area for children

More Goods: property shop, hairdresser, leather goods, shoppers' restaurant, jewellers

① (standard, express & wide checkouts for disabled

BACK

~~INSIDE BACK COVER~~ — leave 1½" (39mm) clear down the right-hand side for photographs

EXCEPTIONAL FOOD RANGES:

Produce: including a wide range of exotic fruit & veg; organically-grown produce.

Meat: huge range includes gourmet cuts, barbecues (special cuts & marinaded meats), licenced for game & venison

In-store Bakery: wide range of cream cakes; 65 different types of bread.

Health Foods: We have the best range of health foods of any store in the area.

Fresh fish: including freshwater & seawater varieties & crustaceans

INSIDE BACK COVER

UNBEATABLE OPENING OFFERS: Household goods/Gardening and DiY/Record, Cassette and CD Players/Food Prices Slashed/Money-off Coupons. — each of these on a new line please

Complete the slip below for your free money-off coupon booklet, and send to Freeway Offers, FREEPOST, London, EC4Y OUQ

Ref: FY4114

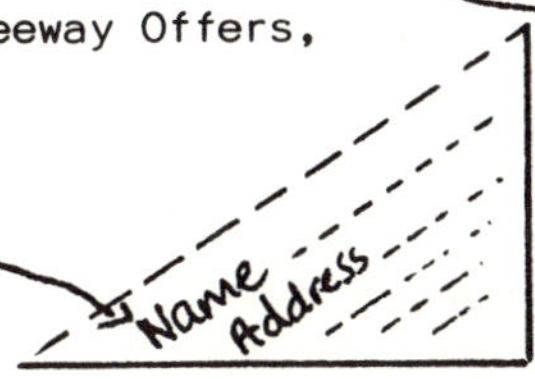

place in r-h corner of the back

3.3 Punctuation is never inserted after a heading, or at the end of a line in displayed work (notice, menu, etc) unless the last word is abbreviated and full punctuation is being used.
3.4 **Never** put full stops in the 24-hour clock; eg 1830 hours.
3.5 The 12-hour clock requires a full stop even when using open punctuation; eg 2.45 pm.
3.6 Full stops are always inserted within decimal enumerations; for example 2.4.1.

Quotation marks

Used when typing direct speech; eg Tom said, 'I must catch the 8.30 train this evening.' Quotation marks are usually placed after the comma, question mark and exclamation mark, eg 'Will I see you tomorrow?' The full stop is placed inside the final quotation mark unless the sentence ends with a title in quotation marks or a single word quotation. For example, 'I will see you at the meeting.' June bought me a copy of 'The Times'.

When two or more paragraphs are quoted, the quotation marks are placed at the **beginning of each paragraph** and at the **end of the last paragraph** only.

These are seldom used in **poetry** except when a line of poetry runs on with the prose. If they are inserted, they are placed at the beginning of the first verse and at the end of the last verse.

With **ellipsis** there is a space after the initial quotation mark and before the first dot, and a space after the third dot and before the final quotation mark.

Rate of production

In business, time represents money, and your employer will expect you to complete your typing as quickly as possible; obviously, all documents must be mailable, ie error free. When training, it is important for you to know whether your speed, accuracy and typing techniques are equal to that demanded by an examining body/employer. Certain examining bodies require candidates to attempt all questions; therefore, we have suggested the approximate number of minutes you should spend on each task so that you complete the **integrated production typing** in $2\frac{1}{2}$ hours. See also ***Integrated production typing***, pages 24–25.

Rearrangement of material

See ***Modification and rearrangement of material***, page 131.

Reports

A business report may be a simple inter-office memorandum about the background of a would-be customer, or it may run into hundreds of pages and be as formal as a comparison of the relative merits of several proposed sites for a new factory, complete with facts and figures presented in tabular form. The formal report may be drafted and rewritten several times.

The aim of any report is to provide information and, while an executive would prepare the report, it is usual for the typist to be responsible for the layout and for the details of style.

Whether short or long, the report is usually divided into sections and subsections and, when it contains a great deal of statistical information, it is easier to understand the information if it is arranged as a table.

The formal report will have a **title** and there may be a cover page and a title page. Then follow the various sections of the report.

1 **Terms of reference**—why and for whom the report has been prepared.
2 **Procedure**—the method used to collect the information.
3 **Findings**—the results of the investigation—should be clearly set out with enumerated headings and subheadings.
4 **Conclusions**—a summary and analysis of the findings.
5 **Recommendations**—what action should, or should not, be taken; these should be individually numbered.

Headings

Most formal reports contain headings that introduce each main division or subdivision. Co-ordinate headings should be typed exactly alike throughout the report.

Style

Consistency in style is also essential. For example, if at the beginning of a report business titles are typed in capitals, then they should not be typed in lower case later on. Or, if a term is abbreviated, it should be abbreviated throughout.

The style you follow will be determined by your employer's preference. Many business firms provide typists with a typing manual and the instructions contained therein must be followed closely. Number every page of a report uniformly.

Spacing

If you are typing a draft, type this word in capital letters at the top left margin of the first page and use

TECHNIQUE DEVELOPMENT

Read the instructions for each exercise carefully before beginning.

1 *Leaving space for a photograph or diagram*

Using A5 portrait paper, rule a box 60 mm × 60 mm, as shown below. Type down the left-hand side of the box keeping two or three clear spaces between the right-hand edge of your typing and the left-hand edge of the box.

Salesmen usually have a large
territory to cover - but not Adrian
Howarth (pictured right). He sells
to shops in an area of just 4 sq
miles. This doesn't mean he isn't
busy - for his area is a chunk of
Central London with hundreds of
kiosks, newsagents & other small
outlets. Adrian has been with the
co for just 4 mths. On the his daily
route-march through the city he carries a large street map & a
monthly underground rail pass - altho' often, most of his day is
spent on foot, walking the streets from shop to shop.

2 *Drawing boxes for forms*

(a) Draw three boxes 5 mm square horizontally.

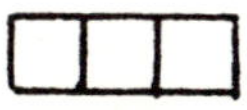

(b) Draw three boxes 5 mm square vertically.

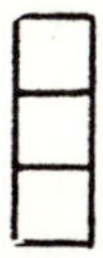

(c) Draw two boxes, 5 mm apart, vertically.

(d) Draw two boxes 10 mm square.

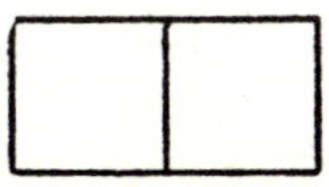

(e) Cross-hatch the right box.

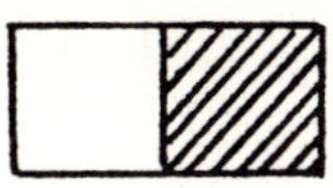

(f) Draw three sides of a box 30 mm × 20 mm.

(g) Insert paper into your typewriter to type the vertical dashed line.

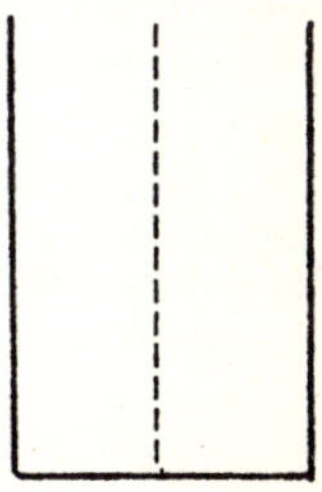

Proofreading

Proofreading is not easy. Our eyes have a way of passing over the line of typescript and seeing what the mind thinks is there, and not what the fingers actually put there. Moreover, the time devoted to proofreading appears to be non-productive and the typist may feel that his or her time would be better used in getting on with another job. Yet proofreading is the sole responsibility of the typist.

We cannot stress too strongly the necessity of reading through your typescript and making any alterations before removing the document from the typewriter.

There are several common types of errors for which you should look:

1 Word substitution: FROM for FORM, IS for IT, AS for IS, IN for ON, YOU for YOUR.
2 Transposition of letters: r and t, v and b, i and e— and substitutions that are difficult to detect: n for m, d for s, u for y, or vice versa.
3 Omission of a line, or lines, which does not outwardly affect the meaning. Check finished work with original.
4 Wrong choice of words when there are two or more words of similar sound, such as plain, plane; all ready, already; advice, advise.
5 Inconsistencies.
6 Names, addresses and figures need special attention.

Proportional spacing

With proportional spacing, the characters do not all take up the same amount of space. As in printing, each character is given its natural width. For example, an n is wider than an i, an m is wider than an n and a capital M is wider than a lower-case m. The characters are not measured in spaces but in terms of units. One of the outstanding features of proportional spacing is that the typed copy appears to be printed rather than typed.

Punctuation

1 Open

Many organizations are now using open punctuation in a variety of documents. This is particularly so in business letters. Note the following when using open punctuation:

1.1 Grammatical punctuation must still be used.
1.2 Where an abbreviation ends in a full stop, the full stop is omitted and replaced by a space. Example: Mrs (space) A (space) W (space) Gurney, senior partner in Messrs Gurney & Asquith, will discuss the change of trading name to W R Holt & Co Ltd, etc, when she calls tomorrow.
1.3 Where abbreviations consist of two or more letters with full stops after each letter, the full stops are omitted and no space is left between the letters, but one space is left after the group of letters; eg John R Jamieson Esq MBE MP.
1.4 When typing a **business letter** with open punctuation, **no** punctuation at all is inserted in the reference, date, name and address of addressee, or salutation; nor following the complimentary close and any wording below. Similarly, when addressing an **envelope** in open punctuation, **no** punctuation is inserted; eg

OPEN

John R Jamieson Esq MBE MP
97 Stirling Road
STAFFORD
ST17 1JP

FULL

John R. Jamieson, Esq., M.B.E., M.P.,
97 Stirling Road,
STAFFORD.
ST17 1JP

1.5 In continuous matter, where the name and address 'run on', the parts are separated by commas, or an extra space.
1.6 Full stops are omitted after figures used in enumerated items.

2 Full

Full stops are inserted after abbreviations as follows:

2.1 Mrs. (space) A. (space) W. (space) Gurney, senior partner in Messrs. Gurney & Asquith, will discuss the change of trading name to W. R. Holt & Co. Ltd., etc., when she calls tomorrow.
2.2 John R. Jamieson, Esq., M.B.E., M.P.

3 Notes

3.1 Certain abbreviations and acronyms may be typed without full stops even when using full punctuation. Here are a few examples: VAT, NATO, PAYE, UK, USA, RSA, LCCI, BBC, etc.
3.2 No punctuation is inserted in abbreviations used for metric measurements even when using full punctuation unless it is the end of a sentence; eg A4 paper measures 210 × 297 mm. Full stops should be inserted in imperial measurements when typing with full punctuation; eg Messrs. J. R. Smith & Co. asked for six doors each measuring 6 ft. 4 in. × 3 ft. 5 in.

SKILL BUILDING 3

1 *Alphabetic sentences* Type each sentence twice.

The morning journey proved exceptionally difficult with quantities of black ice, freezing fog and strong winds.

With the new jig equipment fully installed, potential workplace hazards are expected to drop to a more acceptable level.

2 *Improve control of words with common prefixes*

provide procedure promotion production profitable protection proposal

disappoint discussion discount dismiss dispatch display distinction

consequence convenient confident confirm conscious conflict connection

performance personal personnel percentage periodic permanent persist

exchange exclude execute excuse expand expenditure extensive extract

3 *Improve control of top row keys*

writer tyre worried quote riot party pretty utter query equip

typewriter opportunity popularity equator rapture priority utopia

4 *Improve control of bottom row drills*

numb zinc vaccine brazen manic Manx maize venom vacuum box mix

minimum vacancy excommunicate maximize backbone movement backbench

5 *Skill measurement* Target time for each exercise is 1 minute, not more than 1 error.

The key to our future success lies in the quality and effectiveness of our senior management and their ability to adapt positively and rapidly to meet the future. Major emphasis is placed upon the delivery of timely, efficient services to our customers.

250 keystrokes (50 words)

Dutch tourists on a visit to London attempted to gain access via the Members' entrance to the House of Commons. They were stopped by a constable 'You can't come in here', he bellowed, before adding 'I'm only shouting because you're foreign.'

250 keystrokes (50 words)

Proofreaders' marks

When amendments have to be made in typewritten or handwritten work of which a fair copy is to be typed, these may be indicated in the original copy by proofreaders' marks. To avoid confusion, the mark may also be placed in the margin against the line in which the correction is to be made. Certain examining bodies use only the stet signs, ie ⊘ in the margin, but other examining bodies may use any or all of the examples that follow.

Mark which may be in margin	*Meaning*	*Mark in text*	
lc	Lower case—small letter(s).	— /	Under letter(s) to be altered or struck through letter(s).
uc or CAPS	Upper case—capital letter(s).	═ /	Under letter(s) to be altered or struck through letter(s).
∂	Delete—take out.	/	Through letter(s) or word(s).
NP or //	New paragraph.	// or [	Placed before the first word of a new paragraph.
Stet or ⊘	Let it stand, ie type the word(s) that has been crossed out and has a dotted or broken line underneath.	----	Under word(s) struck out.
Run on	No new paragraph required. Carry straight on.	⟵⟶	
⋏	Caret—insert letter, word(s) omitted	⋏	Placed where the omission occurs.
⁀	Close up—less space.	⁀	Between letters or words.
trs	Transpose, ie change order of words or letters as marked.	⟲ ∽	Between letters or words, sometimes numbered.
#	Insert space.	⋏	
‖	Straighten margin.		
ital.	Italic	—	(Underscore)
⊙	Insert full stop.	⋏	
;/	Insert semi-colon.	⋏	
⦂	Insert colon.	⋏	
,/	Insert comma.	⋏	
ʼ/	Insert apostrophe.	⋏	
H	Insert hyphen.	⋏	
|-|	Insert dash.	⋏	
“/ ”/	Insert quotation marks.	⋏	
#	Insert space.	⋏	
⋏	Insert words.	⋏	
(⋏)⋏	Insert brackets.	⋏	

If a word is not clear in the text, it may be written in the margin in capitals. The word should be typed in lower case, or as indicated in the original script.

Exercise 1

Type the following exercise on a postcard. Make sure you leave at least one clear linespace above all the dotted lines. Draw the boxes with pen and ruler after you have finished.

```
GORING DISTRICT COUNCIL                    Date as Postmark

POST APPLIED FOR ...............................

POST REF NO [ | | | ]

I ack rec of yr application for the above post.
Please note that in the interests of economy we sh not write
to you again unless you are shortlisted.

Signed ........... Date ...........
```

(Take the last sentence from DataFiles, filename STAND Sp1, page 103)

Exercise 2

Type the following form letter on plain paper in double spacing. Leave 14 lines clear at the top of the page. Draw the boxes with pen and ruler when you have finished.

VIDEO PRESENTATIONS LTD

(use indented paragraphs)

This yr sees the launch of a variety of new & exciting training videos for bus. [New programmes in the 'Management Skills' series include XI - Negotiating Tactics, XII - Staff Counselling, & an update on III - Appraising Technical Staff. [We have arranged preview sessions at a number of UK centres. To book yr place, simply complete the slip below & return to us by 12 Jan (add yr)

- -

(Video Presentations Ltd, Freepost, London, NW1L 4GT) CAPS

Please reserve .... places on yr video preview sessions, as follows.

☐ London, 14 Feb		☐ Birmingham	7 March
☐ Cardiff, 17 Feb		☐ London	17 Mar
☐ Glasgow, 24 Feb		☐ Brighton	18 Mar
☐ Manchester 6 Mar		☐ Bristol	21 Mar

Name .... Co ....

Address ....

....

Telephone No .... Job Title ....

Key in exercise 2 (filename VIDEO) for 10-pitch printout. Use the repeater function for the leader lines, the continuous hyphens to mark the tear-off portion and the indent function/indent tab setting for the indented paragraphs. When you have completed this task, save under filename VIDEO. Recall the document and follow the instructions for text editing on page 100.

2 Headings such as:

PRESS RELEASE

JOHNSTONE & TARRANT PLC
30 Warwick Lane
EDINBURGH EH14 1BY

LOGO

Release: Immediate—10 December 1990

For further information contact:
Marjory Dolphin
Director of Public Relations
Telephone: 031–442 2736

NEW SHOWROOMS IN BIRMINGHAM

3 Wide margins—seldom less than: left 38 mm ($1\frac{1}{2}$ inches) right 25 mm (1 inch).
4 The subject heading should be short and factual.
5 Double spacing for body of the release.
6 Leave two clear spaces between paragraphs (turn up three singles).
7 First paragraph is normally blocked; other paragraphs indented. The indentation is often just two spaces as seen in newspaper columns and printed matter.*
8 On second and subsequent sheets type heading at the right-hand side about 25 mm (1 inch) from the top; at the bottom of each page type the word MORE or CONTINUED in the usual place at the right margin.
9 The word (ENDS) is typed, usually in brackets, at the end of the final paragraph.
10 Do not underscore any wording (for emphasis) as to the printer this means italic.

* The release display should follow, as far as possible, standard newspaper conventions, rather than typewriting conventions.

Programme

See ***Folded leaflets***, page 121.

Exercise 3

Type the following form on A4 plain paper. Leave one character space before beginning each row of dots.

APPLICATION ~~FORM~~ FOR LEAVE OF ABSENCE

Failure to complete this form accurately will result in ~~the~~ a delay in granting your leave of absense.

~~You must allow a minimum of 5 working days for processing by Personnel~~

Name................................Department ....

PERIOD REQUIRED: From ....To ....

TOTAL NO ~~NUMBER~~ OF WORKING DAYS ....

REASON FOR LEAVE

☐ ANNUAL HOLIDAY (complete section 2)

☐ STUDY LEAVE (attach form SOL 011)

☐ TIME OFF IN LIEU (attach form TOL 029)

~~SPECIAL LEAVE (attach form S11 40)~~

align at right margin

Sig .... Date ....

SECTION 2

Annual Holiday ~~Holiday~~ Entitlement (including

.... days carried forward ....

APPROVED AND NOTED

Sig........................... } Departmental Manager

Date .... }

HAVE YOU CHECKED THE ACCURACY OF THIS FORM YES/NO

draw a square

RULE THE BORDER AROUND THE FORM AFTER YOU HAVE FINISHED

and cast in capitals. Type in double spacing and centre vertically and horizontally in typing line as in first page. Sometimes list of costumes is included on this page.

4 **Start of play. Page 1**
   4.1 Dropped head for act and act number, ie leave 51 mm (2 inches) at top of paper. May be centred in typing line, ie margins elite 19–94 (centre point 56), pica 16–77 (centre point 46).
   4.2 Turn up two single spaces and type the name of the play etc, as in 4.1.
   4.3 Margins for body of play—left 76 mm (3 inches), right 13 mm ($\frac{1}{2}$ inch).
   4.4 Names of characters: In capitals, starting 38 mm ($1\frac{1}{2}$ inches) from left edge of paper; set tab stop here and use margin release when typing names of characters.
   4.5 Scene directions: Block at left margin.
   4.6 Speeches: Block at left margin.
   4.7 Unspoken words are underscored.
   4.8 Numbering of pages: Pages numbered consecutively at top right side, leaving 13 mm ($\frac{1}{2}$ inch) at top of page. Turn up two single spaces after number before starting to type. Number may be just page, eg 2, or –2–. It may include the act and scene number, eg 1–1–2 = Act 1, Scene 1, page 2.

Poetry

The following points are a guide to the typing of poems:

1 Positioning

The longest line of the verse should be centred on the page or typing line.

2 Spacing

Single spacing, double between verses.

2.1 If alternate lines rhyme, these usually begin at the same scale-point (unless they are of irregular length, when they are centred). The first line and all lines rhyming with it are typed at the margin, while the second and all lines rhyming with it are indented two spaces from the start of the first, third, etc, lines. (Short lines may be indented more than two spaces.)
2.2 In blank verse (ie where no lines rhyme) all lines start at margin.
2.3 When lines are of approximately equal length, and when successive lines rhyme, these start at the margin, ie there is no indentation.
2.4 If all lines rhyme, these all start at the margin.

3 Capitalization

Each line starts with a capital letter.

4 Poet's name

The last letter of the poet's surname ends at the same scale point as the last letter of the longest line.

5 Quotation marks

These are seldom used in poetry except when a line of poetry runs on with the prose. If they are inserted, they are placed at the beginning of the first verse, and at the end of the last verse.

6 Refrain

Typed at least five spaces to the right of the start of the verse(s).

Postcards

Many firms send postcards (A6—[148 mm × 105 mm] [$5\frac{7}{8}$ inches × $4\frac{1}{8}$ inches]) in acknowledgement of letters and orders. These formal acknowledgements are typed like memos with no salutation and no complimentary close.

Note the following points:

1 Centre and type firm's name and address, starting four spaces from top of card.
2 Use margins of five spaces on either side.
3 Always use single spacing with double between paragraphs. Paragraphs may be indented or blocked.
4 After typing address, turn up two single spaces and at left margin insert the reference. On the same line, backspace from right margin and type date.
5 Turn up two single spaces and type body.
6 Type recipient's name and address on reverse side, parallel to the longest edge.

Postscripts

See ***Business letters**, **4.13***, page 110.

Press releases (publicity releases)

Every business firm seeks favourable publicity. One way that a business gets coverage in newspapers and other media is by issuing press releases, sometimes called publicity releases, to news services. Announcements to the media about new products, executive promotions, new showrooms, mergers, etc, are common examples.

Most organizations have their own 'house' style; however, the following is considered to be acceptable:

1 Plain bond paper—type on one side only; very often special paper is used.

Exercise 4

Type the following form on A5 plain paper.

DESKTOP PUBLISHING REQUEST Re-order UM/44

[(leave 5 clear linespaces)]

Name . . . .

Department . . . . Extension . . . .

Authorizing sig . . . .

Disk No. . . . . Doc ~~Ref~~ ref . . . .

Approx total no of pages . . . .

Photographs YES/NO (Please delete as applicable)
[If yes, please ~~attach~~ supply clear (b/w) originals for scanning] (black & white)

(retain square brackets)

END PRODUCT (please tick one only)

A5 folded leaflet		form	
A4 sheets (single spaced)			
column newsletter		p Pressrelease	

Draft required by . . . .

Sig . . . . Date . . . . . .

Paragraphing

1 Styles

There are three different styles of paragraph layout:

1.1 **Indented** The first line usually starts on the sixth space to the right of the second and subsequent lines of the paragraph. You should indent at least five clear spaces before starting to type the first line of the paragraph.

1.2 **Blocked** or **flush** All lines start at the same point on the scale.

1.3 **Hanging** The second and subsequent lines of the paragraph are typed two spaces to the right of the first line.

2 Spacing between paragraphs

2.1 **All** paragraphs typed in **single** spacing have **one** clear space between each paragraph, ie turn up two singles between each paragraph.

2.2 **Indented** and **hanging** paragraphs typed in **double** spacing have **one** clear space between paragraphs, ie turn up one double between each paragraph. In other words, the whole exercise is typed in double spacing.

2.3 When **blocked** paragraphs are typed in double spacing, leave two or three clear spaces between each paragraph, ie turn up three single or two double spaces between each paragraph. A minimum of two clear spaces must be left between paragraphs typed in double spacing.

Personal letters

1 Personal business letters

Used when writing to an unknown person or firm about a personal business matter. The layout is similar to that of a business letter. If your home address is not printed on your stationery, type it about 13 mm ($\frac{1}{2}$ inch) from the top at the left margin, or centred on page, or in such a way that the last line ends flush with the right-hand margin. Date in usual place. Name and address of addressee may be typed in usual place or two spaces below your name at the left margin.

2 Formal personal letters

Used when writing to someone older than yourself or to whom you owe respect. Layout as for personal business letter. Salutation is formal, eg Dear Miss Brown, Dear Mrs Taylor, Dear Mr Emery.

3 Personal letters

Used when writing to a personal friend. Your address and date as in a personal business letter. No name and address of addressee. Salutation is informal, eg Dear Mary, Dear Arthur, Dear Uncle George.

NOTE: It is now fairly common practice not to use titles when writing to personal friends; therefore, when corresponding with your close friend Anne Crawford or John Taylor, you would not use Ms, Miss, Mrs or Mr. We suggest that you exercise great care so as not to offend the more mature or pedantic person!

Photocopying

See ***Reprography***, page 140.

Pitch

This refers to the spacing of the typewriter and the space taken up by a typewritten character. The most common sizes are 10 and 12 pitch—10 pitch = 10 characters to the inch; 12 pitch = 12 characters to the inch. Originally, a typewriter was either 10 pitch (pica typeface) or 12 pitch (elite typeface), but with electric typewriters using golf ball heads, we moved on to machines with dual pitch, which meant that by fitting the appropriate head and by the movement of a lever, you could type in 10 **or** 12 pitch. Most electronic typewriters have 10, 12 and 15 pitch; however, on the more sophisticated machines there is a greater variety of pitches including proportional spacing (PS).

Golf ball heads and daisywheels are now available in a great many typefaces and pitches which include technical, chemical, mathematical and optical character recognition elements.

Plays

Although the layout of plays may vary according to individual preference, the following points are generally acceptable and will be a guide to you. In a typewriting examination you should follow the general layout and instructions given.

1 Size of paper: A4.

2 Binding margin of 38 mm ($1\frac{1}{2}$ inches).

3 **Introductory pages**
These are not usually numbered. The arrangement is as follows:
First page—Title page: Title and type of play and author's name usually in capitals. May be centred vertically and horizontally in typing line, taking into account the binding margin, ie elite 19–94 (centre point 56), pica 16–77 (centre point 46).

Second page—Synopsis of acts and scenery: Acts and numbers of acts in capitals. May be centred vertically and horizontally in typing line as on first page above.

Third page—List of characters: Typed in capitals. If cast is included, characters are in lower case

Exercise 5

Type the following form on A5 paper (for 12-pitch typeface) or on A4 paper (for 10-pitch typeface).

ADVERTISING PRODUCTION REQUEST ← (Spaced caps)

Name . . . . Department . . . .

Location . . . . Employee No . . . .

Telephone . . . . Authorizing Sig . . . .

Description/title of job* . . . .

. . . .

. . . .

Required Measurements				FOR OFFICE USE
Width (cm)	Depth (cm)	Publication	Date of Insertion	Date Rec'd . . . . . Cost £ . . . . . Charge Code ☐☐

Approx Cost (including VAT) . . . .

* (Take from DataFiles, filename STAND Sp2, page 103)

(Retain Rec'd as an abbreviation please)

between each group. Set left margin and tab stops for the start of each column. It is usual to return once before, and twice after, a horizontal line but, more, or less, space may be left.

Exercise 4, on page 58, is a simple form of the centred style. Exercise 5 is also centred, but is a little more complicated. Centre *Plant Manager* in the usual way; then backspace (one for every two characters and spaces) from the centre point of the paper for the longest words in the last two lines, allowing three spaces between each group of items. Set a left margin and the tab stops. It is sometimes easier to insert the typed horizontal line after you have typed the items beneath it.

Pagination

This means the numbering of pages. The first page is not usually numbered, second and subsequent pages are numbered 13 mm ($\frac{1}{2}$ inch) (turn up four single-line spaces) from the top edge of the paper, in arabic figures. The number may be blocked at the left or right margin or centred on the typing line. Some business houses prefer to have the pages numbered at the bottom.

Paper

Different qualities and weights of typing paper are available: plain bond, letterhead, bank, duplicating, etc. Most businesses use a good quality bond for their letterheads (except for airmail letters, when a light-weight paper is used) and a similar quality of plain bond paper for continuation sheets and top copies of documents.

Carbon copies are normally typed on a thin paper known as bank (flimsy); it is also available in a variety of weights and qualities. Many organizations prefer an inexpensive coloured paper for carbon copies.

Stencil duplicating paper is usually a soft, porous paper into which the ink quickly penetrates and dries.

Paper sizes—reference table

Paper	Size		Horizontal spacing						Vertical spacing
			Number of horizontal spaces			Centre point of paper			Total number of single-line spaces
			Pitch			Pitch			
	Millimetres	Inches	10	12	15	10	12	15	
International									
A4 portrait	210 × 297	$8\frac{1}{4} \times 11\frac{3}{4}$	82	100	124	41	50	62	70
A4 landscape	297 × 210	$11\frac{3}{4} \times 8\frac{1}{4}$	117	141	176	58	70	88	50
A5 portrait	148 × 210	$5\frac{7}{8} \times 8\frac{1}{4}$	59	70	88	29	35	44	50
A5 landscape	210 × 148	$8\frac{1}{4} \times 5\frac{7}{8}$	82	100	124	41	50	62	35
A6 postcard	148 × 105	$5\frac{7}{8} \times 4\frac{1}{8}$	59	70	88	29	35	44	25
$\frac{2}{3}$ A4 portrait	210 × 198	$8\frac{1}{4} \times 7\frac{4}{5}$	82	100	124	41	50	62	47

Exercise 6

Type the following form on A4 plain paper. Make sure that you leave sufficient space for completion of all details.

SICKNESS CERTIFICATE (Mr/Mrs/Ms)

Surname . . . . First Name (s) . . . .

Group/Department . . . . . Location . . . .

Telephone No . . . . Extension . . . .

Date of last absence

I (hereby) certify that I was unable to attend work:

From . . . . to . . . .

because I was suffering from . . . .

(allow 2 more lines of dots)

Did you consult a doctor or attend a hospital* YES/NO

(Plse delete as applicable)

If yes, please give the name of yr doctor or hospital . . . .

DECLARATION

I understand th to give false info on this certificate is an abuse of the sick pay scheme and will render me liable to disciplinary action.

SIGNED . . . . Date . . . .

Countersigned . . . . Date . . . .

(Notes of Discussion) CAPS — allow min of 1¾" or 45 mm for depth.

* Attach original of doctor's note

Notice of annual general meeting and agenda of public limited companies

Usually typed in blocked style with open or full punctuation. The wording is more formal than that used in other notices and agendas. In addition to the notice and agenda, certain other information (where applicable) is given about: voting rights, proxy votes and forms, directors' service contracts, directors' shares and debenture interests, etc.

Notice of meetings

For formal meetings, such as general meetings, extraordinary general meetings, and committee meetings, written notices are sent to those entitled to attend. The notice, which is prepared by the secretary, should contain details of the date, place and time of meeting. The salutation and complimentary close may be omitted. They may be typed in centred or blocked style with open or full punctuation.

Numbers

1 Cardinal numbers

These are arabic numbers—1, 2, 3, etc.

1.1 The figure 1 is expressed either by the lower-case l or by the figure 1 if this is provided on the typewriter, but these must not be mixed, ie the same key must be used for figure 1 throughout an exercise. **Never** use capital I for the cardinal number 1.

2 Ordinal numbers

Denote order or sequence, eg 1st, 2nd or first, second.

2.1 These are not abbreviations and must not, therefore, be followed by a full stop.

2.2 Words or figures may be used: follow the script and be consistent—either words or figures.

3 Roman numerals

These are formed from seven symbols known as units and fives, viz:

3.1	Units	I (1)	X (10)	C (100)	M (1,000)
3.2	Fives		V (5)	L (50)	D (500)

4 Figures in columns

4.1 Units under units, tens under tens, etc.

4.2 Thousands, etc, should be marked either by a comma or space—be consistent.

5 Figures in continuous matter

5.1 Four digits—thousands marked by comma or typed close up—4,582, 4582; preferable always to use the comma.

5.2 Five or more digits, thousands **must** be marked by commas—28,372, 613,924.

5.3 If a task contains groups of five or more digits, then any four digit figures, in the same task, **must** have a comma separating hundreds and thousands.

5.4 Always be consistent when typing figures; eg type 20,000 not 20 thousand; type 300 not 3 hundred.
EXCEPTION It is acceptable to type £3,000,000 or £3m or £3 million, but it would seem preferable always to use figures.

5.5 Thousand(s) may be represented by K, eg 24K equals 24,000.

Offset-litho

See ***Reprography***, page 140.

Organization charts

An organization chart shows the various departments in a business (in a large establishment it could be details of the structure of one department or even a section of a department) and sets out lines of communication, delegation and authority.

By studying an organization chart, one can see the responsibilities of each department and to whom each department is responsible. Usually, but not necessarily, top management is at the head of the chart and the connecting lines lead downwards to lower management.

The layout and style of organization charts vary considerably, and each one should be studied and planned before typing starts. A chart may be blocked at the left margin or centred, typed on A5 or A4 paper, and the linespacing can vary from chart to chart. The lines may be ruled by underscore, by ink, or a combination of both, provided that the ink is the same colour as the underscore lines. It is usual to leave three clear character spaces between separate items.

The organization chart shown on page 57, exercise 1, has been blocked and is a simple form of display. When typing exercise 2, which also is in blocked style, it will be necessary to backspace from the centre point of the paper for the longest words of the last two lines together with the word *Accountant*, plus half the number of the spaces that will be left

Exercise 7

Type the following table on A4 landscape paper. Read through carefully before beginning.

HOW TO ORDER

1. Choose what you wd like from the enclosed sales cat & fill in the order form, indicating a 2nd colour choice if poss. To prevent delays check that the code section has been correctly completed.

2. Fill in the section headed 'Payment Details' & post in the envelope provided to us.

(typist - Leave an area at least 2" (51mm) across x 1½" (39mm down) blank

Please make sure you print yr details on the address label below:

NAME

ADDRESS

POSTCODE

Tel No

PAYMENT DETAILS £

Total Value of Goods Ordered (CAPS) ....

\+ postage & packing

Total payment sent (CAPS)

Cheque Value (under these 2 items)

Credit Card Value

Credit Card Details (Access, Visa, Diner's Club, American Express) ....

Expiry Date ....

Sig ....

Card No (16 boxes needed)

YR ORDER

Description	Cat Page No	1st Colour choice	2nd Colour choice	Size	Order Code	Price per Item £	Total Price £

Memorandum

The memorandum (usually referred to as 'memo') is one of the most convenient ways of sending messages from one person to another in the same firm, or from the head office to a branch office or agent. A memo may be typed on any of the usual sizes of paper, and firms have the headings printed and the paper cut to the size required. The layout of the headings varies.

It is quite common practice to set the left margin to coincide with the beginning of the printed headings, provided it is not less than 25 mm (1 inch). It is preferable not to have the right margin wider than the left margin. The insertions are typed two spaces after the end of the printed headings. It is important that this space is consistent after each heading.

Other points to remember

1 No salutation or complimentary close.
2 **Body** Usually in single spacing with double between paragraphs. Blocked or indented paragraphs must be used consistently.
3 Some firms have the writer's name or initials typed two single spaces after the last line of the body of the memo.
4 If there are printed dotted lines after the printed headings, the insertions must be typed slightly above these, so that the 'long' letters are not touching the dotted lines. If there are no lines, the insertions will be aligned with the printed headings. The variable linespacer will be used in both cases to make sure that the alignment is correct.
5 **Continuation sheets** Always use **plain paper** of the same size, colour and quality as the first page; turn up four single spaces from the top and type the page number, date and the name of the addressee. If blocked paragraphs are used, these details are typed at the left margin in single or double spacing in the following order: page number, date, name of addressee. If indented paragraphs are used, the name of the addressee is typed at the left margin, the page number is centred in the typing line, and the date ends at the right margin. The memo is continued on the third single space below the continuation sheet details. If a continuation sheet is needed, the memo must be so arranged that the matter on the continuation sheet extends at least to a second line. Do not divide a word from one page to the next. The word CONTINUED or PTO may be used in memos. A catchword, ie the typing of the first word of the text appearing on a continuation sheet, is sometimes placed at the foot of the preceding page. The number of the next page must not be used as a catchword.
6 The notation for directing carbon copies is the same as for business letters.
NOTE: Many organizations no longer use courtesy titles for personal names in memoranda. Follow house style or instructions.

Minus and plus signs

These are placed close to the figure to show a minus or plus quantity, eg −78, +22. However, when used to show subtraction or addition, the dash (space either side) and the + sign with a space on either side are used, eg 218 − 118 + 50 = 150. The following is an example of the two uses of the minus sign:

20 − 10 = 10; 10 − 20 = −10.

Minutes of a meeting

Details of any decisions or resolutions, or business discussed at a meeting, are recorded and preserved. These are known as minutes. Each minute is numbered as this facilitates indexing. The order in which the minutes are typed always follows the order in which the items appeared on the agenda.

1 Description of meeting, including time, date and place.
2 Names of those present—chairman's name appearing first, followed by the names of the officers/members.
3 Apologies received.
4 Reading of minutes of last meeting.
5 Matters arising.
6 Correspondence.
7 Reports of officers.
8 General business discussed—with details of any resolutions taken.
9 Any other business.
10 Place, date and time of next meeting.
11 Place for chairman's signature.
12 Date on which minutes are signed.

The minutes may be typed with shoulder headings or side headings in blocked or indented style with either full or open punctuation.

Modification and rearrangement of material

In an office, your employer may give you specific or general instructions about altering the layout of a document, and these instructions should be followed very carefully.

If in an examination you are directed to modify or alter the layout of an exercise, these instructions **must** be followed; otherwise marks will be lost. Before starting to type, thoroughly read through the task and mark the script clearly in ink where any alterations have to be made. For example, if items have to be rearranged in date order, write 1, 2, 3, 4, etc, against the items in the order in which they should be typed. Time spent in preparation, will lead to greater accuracy and speed in typing.

SKILL BUILDING 4

1 *Alphabetic sentences*

Type each sentence twice.

The jazz band plays here every weekday evening, and sometimes for external venues at lunchtimes if required.

They were subsequently awarded joint first prize for their exceptionally strong performances in the track events.

2 *Improve control of single-hand words*

Using left hand

transverse cabaret cascade cataract beeswax bereaved decrease westward

Using right hand

monopoly hymn knoll July pull hilly yolk lollipop pupil union pony

3 *Improve control of words with common suffixes*

presidency deficiency tendency divergency frequency fluency agency

thoughtful careful mindful plentiful helpful respectful useful

luxurious continuous malicious marvellous nervous conscientious

conformity capacity majority ability diversity disparity technicality

4 *Production development from manuscript*

Reading time: 1 minute   Target typing time: 2 minutes

Career ~~opportunities~~ openings for well-qualified secs remain varied & challenging. In the London area ~~alone~~ their is still a shortage of high calibre secs w shorthand/typing speeds in excess of 90/50, & a sound knowledge of WP; for those w good language skills in French, German, (Italian) or (Spanish), there are openings w the EEC in Brussels & the Foreign Office. The single European market of 1992 shd provide even better opps for those fluent in more than 1 European language.

500 keystrokes (100 words)

3.1 Put a light pencil mark 25 mm (1 inch) from the top and at least 25 mm (1 inch) from the bottom edge of the paper before inserting into the machine; or

3.2 Rule a heavy line on a backing sheet (which is usually wider than the typing paper) across the complete width of the sheet 25 mm (1 inch) from the top, and at a point at least 25 mm (1 inch) from the bottom.

4 **Pagination**—the numbering of pages. The first page is not usually numbered; second and subsequent pages are numbered in arabic figures 13 mm ($\frac{1}{2}$ inch) (turn up four linespaces) from the top edge of the paper. The number may be blocked at the left or right margin or centred on the typing line. Some offices prefer to have the pages numbered at the bottom.

5 Chapter headings—See ***Headings***, page 126.

6 Catchword—See ***Catchword***, page 112.

7 The typist is expected to correct errors in spelling, grammar or punctuation, should these occur in the original draft. Where a word can be spelt in two ways, the same spelling **must** be adopted throughout the document.

8 In any piece of work it is essential that the layout for chapter headings, use of capitals, numbering, etc, is consistent. In fact, it is a good plan only to vary your style where this would improve the layout or where you are instructed to use a particular form of display.

9 **Reverse of paper** If a continuation sheet is typed on the reverse of the paper and the margins used are not equal, the margin settings should also be reversed.

Locating information

See ***Data files***, pages 102 and 115.

Log sheets

See page 24.

Logo

Symbol or trademark of an organization.

Margins

In business, or in an examination, you are seldom given margin settings, and, therefore, you must get accustomed to choosing the most suitable margins for the length of the document and the type of display. See ***Standard margins***, page 144.

If you are given specific measurements (millimetres/inches) for margins—say 25 mm (1 inch) on the left and 13 mm ($\frac{1}{2}$ inch) on the right—then it is better to measure and mark the paper in pencil, before inserting it into the machine and setting the margins.

Measurements

In typing measurements, the following points should be noted:

1 One space is left after the number(s) and before the unit of measurement. Example: 8½ (space) in; 148 (space) mm; 2.5 (space) cm.

2 Do not add an 's' to the symbol to form the plural—symbols are the same in the plural as they are in the singular, eg 20 metres = 20 m; 14 inches = 14 in.

3 When the signs for feet and inches are used, no space is left between the figures and the sign, but one space is left after the sign, eg 2 ft 3 in = 2′ (space) 3″.

4 Full stops are **never** used in abbreviations of metric measurements (except at the end of a sentence) and they should not be used in ft (foot/feet), in (inch/inches), etc, when typing with open punctuation. However, when **full punctuation** is being used, the full stop must be inserted in imperial measurements, eg 3 ft. 4 in. × 6 ft. 9 in. Do not mix the signs (′ and ″) with the abbreviations (ft and in).

5 The letter 'x' (lower case) is used for the word 'by'. Example: 210 mm × 297 mm (space before and after the 'x').

6 At line ends **never** separate the figure(s) from the symbol.

7 Most symbols are small letters, but there are a few in upper case such as C and M which stand for Celsius and mega. Certain keyboards (teleprinters, for example) have upper case letters only, and when using such machines, the unit should be typed in full, eg 15 METRES.

8 As it may cause confusion, the symbols l (lower case L) for litre(s) and t (lower case T) for tonne(s) should not be used—better to write the words in full. If, for some reason, the abbreviation for litre is essential, then insert it in ink and use a looped 'el', ie ℓ.

INTEGRATED PRODUCTION TYPING

These simulated office tasks are preceded by a **typist's log sheet** (copy in the *Workguide and Resource Material*). Refer to the **log sheet** for instructions and relevant details before and during the typing of the documents.

Timing

Today, because of the number of automatic functions on certain electronic keyboards (as compared with, say, a manual typewriter), it is impossible to set an average timing for any one document. In some typewriting examinations it is essential that you attempt all questions; therefore, we suggest that your objective is to type the **integrated production typing** in 2½ hours, and, to help you judge just how much **time you can afford to spend on each task**, we have allocated the maximum number of minutes you should devote to any one task in order to finish the paper within the stipulated time. This time includes proofreading the typed page before removing it from the machine and making corrections where necessary.

Reading the manuscript or typescript through to see that you understand the contents (which is of paramount importance), deciding on linespacing and margins, reading and following instructions, are all essential typing techniques that require immediate decisions and must be carried out speedily and accurately. Therefore, within the timing of 2½ hours, we have left 15 minutes unused so that you can spend the first 10 minutes reading through the complete script, marking the special points to watch for and corrections to be made, deciding on what paper to use, what margins to set, where carbon copies are required, etc, and another five minutes for a final check to see that each task has been attempted and each instruction followed. Of course, it may be that you will take less time than that stated, and this is good as you will then have time in reserve.

Folders

Keep the typed documents in a folder marked FOR SIGNATURE, and the folder (with the tasks in document number order; together with the **log sheet**) should be handed to your teacher when you are sure that all the documents (in any one group) are MAILABLE and ready for approval and signature where appropriate. Also, keep a separate folder for the documents that have been approved/signed—file the documents under the **log sheet** number and in document number order.

Mailable documents

The contents must make sense; no omissions (you could have a serious omission and the document may still make sense); no uncorrected errors (misspellings, incorrect punctuation, typing errors, etc); no careless corrections (if part of the wrong letter(s) is showing, the correction is not acceptable); no smudges; no creases. Consistency in spelling, in format, in typing sums of money, etc, is vital. Occasionally, your teacher may return a document marked C & M (correct and mail). This means that there is an error that will not be difficult to correct, and after a neat correction the document may be mailed.

Typist's log sheet

The information in the **typist's log sheet** will follow a pattern: name of employer will be at the top; the name of the originator and the department (where appropriate) will be handwritten; the date may or may not be given, but letters and memos must have a date unless there are instructions to the contrary. If you have access to a word processor, a text-editing electronic typewriter, or a correction only electronic typewriter, follow the general instructions given on the **log sheet** against the symbol Enter your name, date and starting time near the bottom of the sheet. When all the documents have been completed and are ready for approval/ signature, calculate and enter the TOTAL TYPING TIME at the bottom of the last column and also record the date and time of completion.

Urgent

Note that any input marked with an asterisk (*) is urgent and should be dealt with first.

Linespacing

Usually typed in double spacing.

Folding

A4 documents are folded into two lengthways or into four horizontally.

To fold into two lengthways Place the sheet or sheets face upwards on the table and turn left edge over to meet edge.

To fold into four Place the sheets face upwards on the table, turn bottom edges to meet top, crease flat, then take folded edge, turn upwards and crease again.

Endorsement

When the document is folded, the endorsement is typed on the uppermost side, with the open edges to the right and the fold to the left. The details contain the following information in the order given—date, names of parties, name and description of document.

In a modern legal office, the skeleton form is recorded on the storage media for a word processor. When required, the skeleton form is retrieved and the variables are inserted.

Line-end division

1 General

1.1 If possible, avoid dividing a word at the end of a line.

1.2 If it is necessary to do so in order to avoid an unsightly right-hand margin, you should not divide on more than two consecutive lines.

1.3 Divide according to syllables *provided that the pronunciation of the word is not thereby changed*.

1.4 Wherever possible, let the portion of the word left at the end of the line indicate what the word is.

2 Specific

Divide

2.1 After a prefix and before a suffix. Examples: inter-sect, absorp-tion.

2.2 *Before* the repeated consonant if the final consonant is doubled (to apply spelling rule). Example: shop-ping.

2.3 *After* the repeated consonant if the root word ends in a double consonant. Example: miss-ing.

2.4 Between the two consonants (usually) when a consonant is doubled medially. Example: bag-gage.

2.5 After a single-letter syllable in the *middle* of a word. Example: manu-script.

2.6 Between two *different* consecutive consonants in the *middle* of a word. Example: desig-nation.

2.7 After the first of three consecutive consonants in the *middle*. Example: magis-trate.

2.8 At the original point of junction in compound words and words already hyphenated. Example: fisher-man, pre-eminent.

2.9 Between two separately sounded vowels. Example: radi-ator.

Do not divide

2.10 Words of one syllable or their plurals. Examples: course, courses.

2.11 After one or before two letters only. Examples: again, aided.

2.12 Proper names. Example: Wilson.

2.13 Sums of money, sets of figures, or contracted words. Examples: £14.32, isn't, 123,456,789.

2.14 At a point which alters the pronunciation. Examples: prod-uct (*not* pro-duct), kin-dred (*not* kind-red).

2.15 The last word of a paragraph or a page.

2.16 Foreign words—unless you know the language and where to divide.

NOTE With many electronic keyboards it is not necessary to press the return key at the end of each line to move the cursor down to the beginning of the next line. If the last word does not fit on the line, the system automatically brings the word down to the next line. This is known as wraparound or wordwrap. However, it will be necessary to press the return key for extra linespacing and after short lines, headings, etc.

It may also be possible for your machine to hyphenate a word at the end of the line, but, as the machine does not know the rules for hyphenation, it will insert the hyphen after the last character on the line, whatever it may be, and ask you to make a decision.

Literary work

For the typing of reports, short stories, scripts for books, theses, etc, the following will be a guide:

1 A4 paper is generally used.

2 Linespacing will depend upon the matter to be typed. Follow instructions or house rules.

3 Margins may be equal all round—preferably 25 mm (1 inch). However, if you have to leave a binding or stitching margin, it would be preferable to leave 38 mm ($1\frac{1}{2}$ inches) on the left and 25 mm (1 inch) on the right. To ensure uniform top and bottom margins on each sheet, either:

Stationery requisition

Before starting the **integrated production typing**, you should read it through and decide on the quantity and kind of stationery you will require for all the tasks, and then fill in a **stationery requisition form** which you should hand to your teacher for approval. You will need headed paper for business letters and memoranda; bond white paper for top copies of other documents; bank paper for carbon copies; carbon paper, envelopes, cards, labels, etc. You may allow yourself a few sheets more than you require, but you should in no circumstances give yourself unlimited supplies. Most employers keep a strict control over the use of stationery. In an examination, your supply of typing paper will be limited. Of course, you will have readily available some means for correction of errors, ruler, pen, pencil, dictionary, carbon paper, etc.

Distractions

As an office worker, it is a necessity of life that you should be able to cope with interruptions and distractions which are a normal part of the office scene. Your boss may ask you to make alterations to a script (already in your possession) while you are engrossed in typing an urgent or complicated document; you may be interrupted by the telephone; a client may call to see your boss, etc. You should be sufficiently accomplished to be able to return to your typing unaffected by these distractions. To simulate office conditions, your tutor may interrupt you while you are working on the **integrated production typing** tasks and give you alterations to an exercise, or hand you an additional task: these alterations/additions are in the *Workguide and Resource Material*. Examining bodies may incorporate this form of distraction during a typing examination.

Dates

A business document is of very little use unless it is dated and has a reference as to its origin. Documents, other than letters and memos, are usually dated at the bottom of the last page with the reference either before or after the date. When you are at business, follow the house style. Typewriting examiners for certain boards will penalize you if you date any document (unless there are instructions to do so) apart from letters and memos.

Superfluous wording

If you add a word(s) not in the script, eg a reference in a letter when it is not given, then you may be penalized by the examiner. Similarly, if you insert a line before a footnote and there is no line in the script, then you may be penalized.

Check very carefully to ascertain what the examiner does and does not accept.

Resource material

The *Workguide and Resource Material* is loose-leaf, and record sheets, printed letterheads, forms, form letters, etc, may be copied and these will make your typing much more realistic.

Integrated production typing

See page 24 of this textbook.

Interliner

The interliner lever (sometimes called the ratchet release) releases the platen temporarily from the linespacing mechanism. It may be on the right or left side of the typewriter. Locate it on your machine. When the lever is returned to the original position, the cylinder goes back to the original writing line.

The interliner is used for:

1 Superscripts and subscripts.
2 Double lines underneath totals.
3 Certain combination characters.

Invitations

It is customary to use formal wording when sending out invitations to weddings, coming-of-age parties, etc. The invitations are written in the third person with a blank space left for the insertion of names of the guests in ink. The invitation begins with the name(s) of the writer(s) whose address is placed at the bottom left margin. The date and RSVP are at the lower right margin. Invitations are not signed. The invitation should be placed in an envelope addressed to the recipient.

Italic

The printer uses italic typeface to emphasize certain words (titles of newspapers, books, periodicals, etc) in a printed document. When preparing a typewritten document for the printer, the typist must underscore the words that the printer has to set in italic typeface. Also, when typing from a printed document, the typist must underscore the words that are printed in italic. If you use a single-element typewriter and have an italic printhead, then, of course, you would type the words in italic instead of underlining them.

Itineraries

Appointments itinerary

If your employer has appointments outside the office, an appointments itinerary may have to be prepared for him/her, and thus the person will know exactly where he/she should be at any given time. This schedule of a day's appointments should be typed on a convenient size of paper or, preferably, on a card. There are many ways of setting out an appointments itinerary. The headings may be blocked or centred, and three spaces are left between columns.

Travel itinerary

A travel itinerary usually implies travelling some distance by one or two types of transport and may or may not include certain appointments. Here again, headings may be blocked or centred and three spaces are left between columns.

Justified right margin

The right margin in typewriting cannot be completely regular as in printing, but for purposes of display it may be made regular by adopting the printer's method. This is known as 'justifying', ie the space between words is increased (where necessary) so that the last character in each line is typed at the same scale point.

For this purpose a draft must be typed, making certain that no line extends beyond the point at which the right margin is set. On the draft copy, additional spaces are indicated, so that when the passage is retyped and the additional spaces are inserted all lines will end at the same scale point.

NOTE: It would be wrong to try and justify 'short' lines.

Most word processing machines have a function key that will automatically justify the right margin. See ***Aligned right margin***, page 106.

Labels

See ***Envelopes***, page 119.

Leader dots/leader lines (continuous dots)

See ***Forms: 1 Layout, 2 Form completion***, pages 123–124; ***Tabulation: 5 Leader dots***, page 147.

Leaflets

See ***Folded leaflets***, page 121.

Legal documents (Agreements, Wills)

Margins

Preferably, left 38 mm ($1\frac{1}{2}$ inches), right 13 mm ($\frac{1}{2}$ inch). Short lines are usually filled in with a typed or handwritten line, or sometimes a series of unspaced hyphens.

GRANT ARCHER & ASSOCIATES

This sheet contains instructions that must be complied with when typing the documents. Read the information carefully before starting, and refer back to it frequently.

OFFICE SERVICES – REQUEST FORM

Typist's log sheet

Originator George Parkinson Department PR Manager Date Ext No 93

Typists operating a word processor, or electronic typewriter with appropriate function keys, should apply the following automatic facilities: top margin; carrier return; line-end hyphenation; underline OR bold print (embolden); error correction; centring; any other relevant applications.

Remember to (a) complete the details required at the bottom of the form; (b) enter typing time per document in the appropriate column; and (c) before submitting this **log sheet** and your completed work, enter TOTAL TYPING TIME in the last column so that the typist's time may be charged to the originator.

Document No	Type of document and instructions	Copies – Original plus	Input form¶	Typing time per document	Total typing time Ɏ
1	Bookmark	Top copy only	M/S		
2	Travel Instructions – Type on A5 or a postcard the shorter edge at the top	Top copy only	M/S		
3	Memo to Allen Blake	Top + 2	M/S		
* 4 URGENT	Programme for Training Presenters (Type now)	Top copy only	M/S		
5	Consultant Location Chart (not yet ready – I will let you have it asap)	Top copy only	M/S		
6	Letter to Jenny Diamond + envelope	Top + 2	Compose from notes		
7	Letter to The Manager, Arden House Hotel + envelope	Top + 1	Compose from notes		
			TOTAL	TYPING TIME	

TYPIST – please complete:

Typist's name: Date received: Date completed:

Time received: Time completed:

If the typed documents cannot be returned within 24 hours, the office services supervisor should inform the originator. Any item that is urgent should be marked with an asterisk (*).

¶ T = Typescript AT = Amended Typescript MS = Manuscript SD = Shorthand Dictation AD = Audio Dictation

Ɏ To be charged to the originator's department.

double spacing, it is usual to turn up two double or three single spaces after the subheading to match in with the two or three clear spaces between paragraphs.

7 Punctuation

There is never a full stop after a **subheading**, or after a **main, shoulder** or **side** heading unless the last word is abbreviated and **full** punctuation is being used.

8 Headings with blocked paragraphs

If blocked paragraphs are being used, it is normal practice to use blocked main and subheadings; however, there is no reason why centred headings should not be used with blocked paragraphs, or blocked main and subheadings with indented paragraphs.

Horizontal and vertical display

1 Horizontal display

Headings and displayed items may be centred on the paper or on the typing line. In either case, find the centre point and backspace once for every two letters and spaces that the typed line will occupy (ignore any odd letter) and begin typing at the point to which you have backspaced. To centre THE TOTAL, backspace TH Espace TO TA (ignore the L). Say the letters to yourself as you backspace.

No punctuation is inserted at the end of lines unless the last word is abbreviated and full punctuation is being used.

NOTE: When the paper is inserted so that the left edge is at 0, note the scale point at which the right edge appears; half that number is the centre of the paper. For example: A4 paper extends from 0 to 100 (elite) or 0 to 82 (pica); the centre would be 50 (elite) or 41 (pica). To find the centre point of the typing line, when the margins have already been set, add the margins together and divide by two. For example, with margins of 20 and 85 the centre point of the typing line is, 20 + 85 = 105 ÷ 2 = 52 (ignore fraction left over).

2 Vertical display

2.1 Count the number of lines (including blank ones) that the material will occupy.

2.2 Subtract that figure from the number of line spaces on your paper. On A4 paper there are approximately 70 single spaces; on A5 portrait paper there are 50 single spaces, and on A5 landscape paper there are 35 single spaces.

2.3 After subtracting, divide the remainder by two (ignoring any fraction) to determine on what line to begin typing. For example, to centre eight lines of double-spaced copy on A5 portrait paper:
you need 15 lines, ie 8 typed, 7 blank.

50 − 15 = 35 lines left over.
35 ÷ 2 = 17 (ignore ½). Start to type the matter on the next line (18).

House style

An organization may decide that letters, memos, reports, etc, should be displayed according to certain conventions or style. This would mean that all letters sent to customers and clients would have the same layout. If the organization you work for has a particular house style which differs from your training or preference, you **must** conform to it without deviation.

Hyphen

This is used to replace the word 'to' in certain instances. Examples:

The firm's address was 19–23 North Street. He lived from 1901–1976. This date could also by typed 1901–76, but you must be careful if the dates spread over two centuries, eg 1707–1806 (NOT 1707–06). The dash is also used to replace 'to'.

Income and expenditure account

See ***Financial statements***, page 120.

Inset matter

This refers to matter that has to be typed to the right of the set left margin. It may or may not be inset from the right margin as well. The inset portion starts a minimum of five spaces in from the left margin and there is a clear linespace above and below.

Where the matter is to be inset from both margins, take the following steps:

1 Find the centre point of typing line—add together the scale points at which the margins are set and divide by two.

2 Bring printing point to centre point of typing line and backspace once for every two characters and spaces in the longest line of the matter to be inset. The point reached is the starting point for all items unless indented or hanging paragraphs are being used. Insetting is useful in emphasizing particular aspects of the text.

1 (12 mins)

(Draw a rectangle 5" x 3½" (127 mm x 81 mm))

Please add these details from the letter to Graham Vernon on page 3

Grant Archer & Associates
at
The Money Show
Stand No → Hall No →
Dates: Wed 25 April to
Fri 27 Apr
Times: 1000 to 1950 hrs
(Fri to 1700 hrs)

Info Technology
Management Selection
Co Relocation
Executive Search
Overseas Trade
Distribution
Ergonomics
Training
EFTPOS
EPOS
PR

2 (12 mins)

Travelling to the Money Show ← (emphasize heading)

By Rail
Trains leave every ½ hr from London Euston to B'ham International & the station itself lies within the Exhibition Centre. Visitors from ~~all~~ other routes shd change at B'ham New St.

By Air
Passengers from B'ham International Airport can reach the Exhibition centre via the Maglev link Simply follow the signs at the airport.

(in under 10 mins)

By Car
The NEC is situated conveniently of Junction 4 of the M6. There are excellent car parking facilities & courtesy buses to ferry you to the exhibition complex.

Accom There is a wide~~r~~ range of quality hotels throughout the area. Visitors may be able to obtain special discount rates at certain hotels ~~in the area~~ by calling Expotel on 01-741-4411.

(Please change shoulder headings to paragraph headings.)

1.2 Press the half-space key/bar and hold it down while you type the first letter of the word; then release the half-space key/bar.
1.3 Repeat 1.2 for the remaining letters.

2 Manual machines

2.1 On some typewriters the space bar can be held down to halfspace the carriage. Follow the same procedure as for electric machines above.
2.2 On other machines the backspace key may be used.
   2.2.1 Bring the printing point to the space where the second letter of the erased word was typed.
   2.2.2 Hold down backspacer, type the first letter and then release backspacer.
   2.2.3 Tap space bar once.
   2.2.4 Hold down backspacer, type the second letter, release backspacer and tap space bar once.
   2.2.5 Continue in the same way with the remaining letters to be typed.

Headings

1 Chapter number and heading

The first page of a chapter may be in the form of a **dropped head**, ie the chapter number, heading, etc, start approximately 51 mm (2 inches) from the top edge of the paper. The chapter heading is usually typed two single spaces below the chapter number.

2 Main heading

This starts on the seventh single space from the top edge of the paper. The main heading may be blocked at the left margin or centred in the typing line, and is usually typed in **closed** or **spaced** capitals. It is usual to leave one clear linespace after the main heading before starting the text. However, if the paragraphs are blocked with double spacing, then it is better to turn up three single or two double spaces after the main heading before the start of the text, so that it gives a balanced appearance, matching the two or three clear spaces between paragraphs.

Main and subheadings can be effectively displayed if prominence is given to important lines by the judicial use of (a) spaced capitals (one space between each letter and three spaces between each word);
(b) closed capitals (one or two spaces between each word); (c) underscore for certain words or lines;
(d) emboldening.

Where the main heading 'runs on' into two or more lines, eg:

```
EXTRACT FROM MINUTES OF THE MEETING
HELD ON 3 JANUARY 1989
```

it would seem preferable to type the lines in single spacing.

3 Paragraph heading

These headings may be typed with initial capitals and lower-case letters and underscored, or in closed capitals with or without the underscore. Paragraph headings may be followed by a full stop, a colon, or two clear spaces, when the appropriate spacing must be left after the punctuation mark. These headings may also be typed in 'run on' style where the heading is part of the sentence, but the first few words are underscored or in capitals.

4 Shoulder heading

These are always typed at the left margin and may be in capitals or in lower case with initial capitals, when they may be underscored. There is always a clear space above and below a shoulder heading.

5 Side headings

They are typed inside the left margin position and usually in closed capitals with or without the underscore. When typing side headings the following steps should be taken:
5.1 First decide on left and right margins.
5.2 Set right margin.
5.3 Set a tab stop at the left margin position.
5.4 From the tab stop in 5.3, tap in once for each character and space in the longest line of the side headings, plus three extra spaces.
5.5 Set the left margin at the point reached in 5.4.
5.6 To type the side headings, use the margin release and bring typing point to tab stop set in 5.3.

NOTE When centring main or subheadings in conjunction with side headings, find the centre point by adding together the scale point where the side headings start and the right margin, then divide by two. If you are using an electronic keyboard, you may have the facility for setting a second margin or automatic indent instead of setting a tab stop.

6 Subheading

In addition to the main heading mentioned in 2, there may be a subheading(s) following the main heading. This heading(s) may be typed at the left margin or centred and may be in closed capitals or in lower case with initial capitals and underscored. If the main heading is centred, then it seems wise to centre the subheading(s); otherwise, the subheading will look like a shoulder heading.

There is usually one clear space between the main heading and a subheading and one clear space between the subheading and the start of the text. However, when typing blocked paragraphs with

3 (15 mins)

Memo to Allan Blake, Customer Relations

Please take 2 copies – 1 for file & a blind copy for Audrey Wilkinson. Use closed CAPS for all headings.

CLIENT MAGAZINE

Further to our recent discussions, I have gone ahead & organized the following contributions

April

An article on Bristol as a financial & economic centre. We ~~are~~ have several important clients in the area, & Anne Lewis of Raycroft has agreed to give you an interview.

May

A brief report on Forestry in Scotland, wh I am hoping to persuade Jeremy Young & ~~Gary Jackson~~ Craig Markham of our ~~Oxford~~ Witney office to jointly contribute.

June

Europe in 1992 – Ted O'Dowell from Plymouth has some good ideas on this & shd be contacting you shortly.

July

Overseas property aquisition – Andrew McDonald from our London office has something wh he thinks can be developed, wh focuses on French & Italian holiday areas.

Wd it be possible to have ~~400~~ 200 extra copies of the July issue to distribute at the Royal Show?

TYPIST – please change shoulder headings to side headings for all the months.

dictator/typist's initials

use of the shift key. No space is left between a whole number and a fraction provided on the keyboard, eg $2\frac{1}{2}$, $3\frac{3}{4}$.

When you are required to type fractions that are not provided on the typewriter keyboard, these should be typed in one of two ways.

Sloping fractions

Type ordinary figures with the oblique, eg 5 twelfths = 5/12; 3 sixteenths = 3/16. Where a whole number comes before a sloping fraction, leave one clear space between the whole number and the fraction: examining bodies will not accept a full stop between the number and the fraction.

`Example:  5 3/16.`

Underscore fractions

Type the enumerator above and the denominator below the typing line.

eg $\frac{5}{12}$ $\frac{3}{16}$ $3\frac{5}{12}$. Notice that, in this case, there is no space between the whole number and the fraction. In the third example ($3\frac{5}{12}$) turn up $1\frac{1}{2}$ spaces and type the whole number, turn back half a space and type the enumerator; without turning up, type the underscore; turn up one space and type the denominator. When a piece of typing contains underscore fractions, type it in double spacing.

Fractions that are provided on the typewriter may be used with either sloping fractions or underscore fractions. **Never** use sloping fractions and underscore fractions in the same exercise.

Vulgar fractions

Note the spacing in the following:

$\frac{5}{12} + \frac{3}{6}$	Do not turn up.
$2\frac{5}{12} - \frac{1}{5}$	Turn up $1\frac{1}{2}$ spaces before the whole number. Turn back half a space to insert enumerator.

Fully-blocked and centred styles

When fully-blocked letters were first introduced in *Typing First Course* in 1963, it was more or less taken for granted that everything must be blocked or centred. Over the years, attitudes have changed and it is now somewhat difficult to establish what might be acceptable and what is not acceptable. However, as we have said in previous editions of *Typing First Course*, in order to make certain information more easily found (date on a letter at right margin) and to give parts of a fully-blocked document more emphasis, there seems to be no reason why headings should not be centred, matter inset from left margin or from both margins, date at right margin, etc. In business, follow instructions or the house style; in examinations, follow instructions or layout and endeavour to meet the requirements of the examining board.

Golf ball head

See ***Single-element typewriters***, page 142.

Half-space corrections

In making a correction (you have typed **the** instead of **that**) how can you squeeze in an extra letter? Erase the word you want to replace. You must now move the word half a space to the left so that only half a space precedes and follows it. To do this, you should keep the carriage/carrier from spacing normally. On manual and electric machines you can, by means of the paper release lever, move the paper so that the printing point is half a space to the left of the word you have erased.

Depending on the make of machine, there are several other ways in which you can control the movement of the carriage/carrier.

1 Electric and some electronic machines

1.1 Bring the carriage/carrier to the space before the first letter of the word you have just erased.

4 (25 mins)

~~G— A— & Associates~~

Programme for Training Presenters } (CAPS & u/score these headings)

Are you fed up w. presentations th either send you to sleep or diving for the door?

High on our list of black marks are poorly laid-out rooms – to hot, to cold, too uncomfortable, to dark, too light, too noisy . . .

Next comes ~~wafflers~~ waffling.

[Equally awful are presenters wh waste our time apologizing for being 'no good at presenting'.

[The voice – who wants to listen to voices that drone, whisper or ~~squo~~ squeak & cannot hold our attention?

Why can't presenters get to the point quickly & stick to it?

[Then the jokes – who needs funny or embarrassing jokes in a serious bus ~~conference?~~ presentation?

So how can the average business-man or woman become more professional & make more effective presentations? 1 way is to consult G— A— & Ass. We are a leading authority in bus presentation techniques – ~~on~~ one of our presentation courses you learn:

– how to org & set up the room

– how to interest yr audience – whether you are ~~pree~~ presenting to 10 or 100 others

– controlling yr nerves

– using yr voice effectively

– when to ~~use~~ use humour in yr presentations

– how to create good overhead projector transparencies (OHTs)

– whether to invest in slide projectors, computer hardware & other new technology to enhance yr presentations.

[Courses can be tailored to suit yr own bus.

If this sounds like the help you need, then ring Ann Bray or Tom Dupée at G— A— & Assoc on Cotswold (0451) ~~221163~~ 410847/8

rules for opening & closing yr presentations

All course delegates are given 2 written critiques on there performance & video cassettes of all practice ~~sessions~~ presentations.

(Display on GA headed paper in 2 columns – start your 2nd column as shown.)

that has to be inserted. Obviously, one would leave more space for a person's surname than one would leave for his/her age; similarly, one would leave more space for a person's address than one would leave for his/her forenames. Columns where figures have to be typed must always be wide enough for the number of figures to be inserted.

Items should always be arranged in a logical sequence and related items, such as personal details in an application form, kept together.

At business, you would have a sample of the completed form and, therefore, would know what space to leave for the items to be inserted. In an examination, you may have to use common sense as to how much space should be left blank for an insertion. The form should look neat and well balanced.

Very often there will be lines of continuous dots/underscore on a form to help a person write in the information clearly. When setting out the form, see that there is one clear space after the last typed character and before the start of the continuous dots/underscore, and one clear space after the last dot and before the next typed character. Where continuous dots/underscore are inserted, always use double spacing. One cannot be specific about the amount of space to leave when inserting dotted lines or the underscore; however, the following suggestions should be helpful.

Surname: 51 mm (2 inches), Forename(s): 76 mm (3 inches), Address: 2 complete lines, Postcode: 25 mm (1 inch), Telephone number: 38 mm ($1\frac{1}{2}$ inches), Date: 51 mm (2 inches).

There are one or two cases where there is no space between the typed character and the start of the continuous dots/underscore: after the £ sign and after the letter M for the insertion of the letter(s) in a person's title; eg, £. . . . and M. . . .

2 *Form completion*

When typing over a dotted line/underscore, the insertion should be typed so that the base of a descending character (p, j, y, g) is just above the dotted line/underscore. For example: `go, put`
`go put`
. . . . . .

Where there is no dotted line or underscore, the insertions should be aligned with the bottom of the printed/typewritten words.

Always leave a minimum of one clear space after the printed/typed headings before the start of the insertions. Always be consistent and leave the same space after each printed/typewritten heading in any one exercise. In completing some forms, it is possible to block the insertions at the same scale point in any one particular section.

If letters/words have to be deleted, use the letter X aligned precisely with the characters previously typed.

3 *Automation*

Word processing technology has eliminated many of the difficulties associated with the preparation and completion of forms and form letters. They can now be prepared and stored in a word processing system, corrections and revisions can be made quickly and easily without having to type the document again, and the form, or form letter, can be retrieved and any variables (including name and address of addressee) automatically inserted.

See also ***Standard paragraphs***, page 144.

Forms of address

1 Courtesy titles must always be used when writing to individuals.
2 Use Mr or Esq (never both) when writing to a male person.
3 Rev, Dr or Sir replaces Mr or Esq.
4 Use Messrs when addressing more than one male person.
5 Use The Misses . . . when writing to more than one single lady with the same surname.
6 Address a married lady and a single lady as follows: Mrs L Brown and Miss J Black (if surnames are different) Mrs L and Miss C Brown (if surnames are the same).
7 Do not use a courtesy title with impersonal names or those beginning with 'The'.
8 Do not use a courtesy title for limited or public companies, even if the name includes a personal name.
9 If the abbreviation 'Snr' (Senior) or 'Jnr' (Junior) is used, this comes immediately after the name and before Esq.
10 Letters after a person's name must be arranged in order of importance as follows: (a) Military Decorations; (b) Civil Decorations, eg OBE; (c) University Degrees, eg MA; (d) MP; (e) JP.

NOTE: Use the courtesy title Ms if it is unclear whether a lady is Mrs or Miss, or if you know that a particular correspondent prefers Ms.

Fractions

In addition to the $\frac{1}{2}$, most typewriters have keys with the most commonly used fractions. Examine your typewriter to find what fraction keys it has and practise the use of these, noting which ones need the

6 Letter to Jenny Diamond

(25 mins)

(Address in Data Files, filename ALPHA, page 102)

Same subject heading & 1st paragraph as the letter to Graham Vernon on page 3. Tell her we've carefully looked at everything but have decided to give the work to a local firm. We liked her design but felt that it wld be easier to work with a local firm.

Tell her we're expanding quite a bit at the moment, & have her org in mind for an interesting future project. I'll be in touch again soon. Send a blind cc to Martin Jervis. (Date for next Mon.)

7. Write to Arden House Hotel

(25 mins)

(Address in Data Files, filename ALPHA, page 102)

Confirm my telephone conversation reserving 2 single rooms with private bath for the nights of Wed/Thurs for myself & Eric West. We shall be arriving at about 6 on 25th & could they reserve a table for dinner at 8.30 on that date? Exps to be charged to our a/c Ex/401/779

(dates as in task 1)

(Please sign this yourself & despatch asap.)

The first paragraph of the letter to Graham Vernon, on page 3, should have been saved under filename NEC/1. It should now be copied to form the first paragraph of the letter to Jenny Diamond.

turn up two single spaces between each. Where the typed text is short and there is plenty of white space on the sheet of paper, you may wish to make a more attractive display by leaving the clear space after the text and before the footnote, with the last line of the footnote ending 25 mm (1 inch) from the bottom of the page. Some examining bodies do not always insert a horizontal line before the footnote and, in that case, it may be wise for the examination candidate to omit the line, and we suggest that examining bodies should be asked to make the candidate's position clear. There is no horizontal line before footnotes which follow a tabulated statement.

If the typewriter has an asterisk key, the typed character will be raised half a space, but if a small x and the hyphen key are used, then it will be necessary to use the halfspace mechanism of the typewriter, or the interliner, to raise the mark above the line of typing. All footnote signs should be superscripts if the asterisk key on the typewriter is used. On word processors, there will be a superscript facility for raising characters above the typing line.

When typing a draft of a document which contains a footnote(s), it is helpful to type the footnote on the next line after the reference in the text, with a horizontal line **above** and **below** it. When the final copy has to be typed, the amount of space required for the footnote(s) at the bottom of the page will then be obvious. The *Oxford Dictionary for Writers and Editors* says that copy for the printer may have the footnotes at the bottom of the page or on a separate sheet with reference figures for identification.

Form letters

Many documents, used by business firms, will contain similar information and wording and, in order to save time, form or skeleton letters, containing the **constant** (unchanging) information, are prepared and are duplicated or printed and only the **variable** items (name and address, etc) are inserted by the typist in the blank spaces which have been purposely left to accommodate these items.

The electronic keyboard and the VDU have made production of repetitive text very much easier and more time-saving. The skeleton letter, containing the constant information, is keyed in and stored on a disk. When required, it can be retrieved by pressing a function key and any insertion can be made quickly and easily (there is no difficulty with alignment when you have a VDU) and the completed letter printed out, so that it looks like an original—as distinct from a duplicated or printed document with the variables added.

When typing in the variables, care must be taken to see that the typeface on the machine used for inserting the particulars is the same size and kind as that used in the duplicated portion, and that the ribbon matches in colour and depth the constant information in the letter.

The following steps should be taken when you fill in a form letter:

1. Insert the form letter into the machine so that the first line of the body of the letter is just above the alignment scale.
2. By means of the paper release, adjust the paper so that the base of the entire line is in alignment with the top of the alignment scale (this position may vary with certain makes of machines) and that an 'i' or 'l' lines up exactly with one of the guide lines, or arrows, on the alignment scale/card holder.
3. Set margin stops and paper guide. The margin stops should be set to correspond to the margins already used in the duplicated letter.
4. Turn the cylinder back two single spaces, and, if not already typed, insert salutation at the left-hand margin.
5. Turn the cylinder back a sufficient number of linespaces to provide the correct space for the reference and name and address of the addressee, and the spaces between, to reach the line for the reference and date.
6. Type the reference at left margin.
7. Type the date.
8. Type the name and address of addressee.
9. Insert any details required and delete any unnecessary letters and/or words.
10. Check carefully.
11. When preparing a form letter, always leave sufficient blank space for the details that have to be inserted. In business, this is not always easy to decide and it is better to be over generous. However, if you have a form letter in an examination and have to insert given details, then it is obvious that you should study the insertions when deciding on the number of blank spaces to leave.

See also ***Forms (Automation)***, page 124, and ***Standard paragraphs***, page 144.

Forms

Forms are printed sheets of paper or cards used to record and transmit information. The part of the information that is always the same is typed or printed in order to save time when completing the form.

1 Layout

When setting out a form, be it on paper or on a card, sufficient space must be left for the information

SKILL BUILDING 5

1 *Alphabetic sentences* Type each sentence twice.

The box just contained a dozen small parcels, from an unknown source, to be divided equally amongst the children.

On the first day we took the maximum group score in equestrian show jumping events by a class of our size.

2 *Improve control of single hand words*

Using left hand

gazeteer afterwards reserve adverse drawer extract beverage beware

Using right hand

million minimum opinion join link only imply nylon jump pink

3 *Improve control of words with common suffixes*

requirement agreement management acknowledgement arrangement equipment

condition relation speculation situation delegation derogation

headship entrepreneurship fellowship partnership kinship chairmanship

sensitive tentative effective expressive constructive productive

reasonable mailable viable remarkable suitable negotiable capable

tangible convertible inflexible credible sensible feasible eligible

4 *Skill measurement* Target time for each exercise is 1 minute, not more than 1 error.

Independent Radio has introduced a new rate card effective from 4 January. Spot rates are up by approximately 25 per cent. Peak special value plans are adjusted both in terms of cost and content. The reasons? Hotter competition; higher costs and increased programme budgets.

280 keystrokes (56 words)

Foreign language specialists look to be in growing demand from 1992. However, a major international survey reveals widespread ignorance and complacency amongst the majority of UK organizations, with a complete misunderstanding of how the new single European market might affect them.

280 keystrokes (56 words)

folded, the number of lines to be typed and the range of display required for each page. To avoid confusion, mark all pages quite clearly in pencil before inserting the paper into the machine.

A4 landscape paper folded to give four sheets of A5 portrait paper

FRONT SIDE OF PAPER UNFOLDED

front page—right-hand side
back page—left-hand side

back page left hand	front page right hand

page 2—left side of fold
page 3—right side of fold

page 2 left side	page 3 right side

A4 landscape paper folded into three

page 1	page 2	page 3

reverse side of page 3	reverse side of page 2	front cover reverse of page 1

Front cover

This will contain the title or main points of the document and should be given emphasis by the judicial use of centring, blocking, emboldening, capitals, spaced capitals, underlining, etc, so that the result is neat, attractive and eye catching.

Inside pages

It gives a more pleasing appearance if the far left and far right margins are equal, and where there is sufficient space, the margins on either side of the fold should match the left and right margins; however, this is by no means obligatory as long as there is equal space (say 13 mm ($\frac{1}{2}$ inch)) on either side of the fold. It will give a more balanced appearance if the display on each page starts at the same distance from the top. The inside page where the display takes up most vertical space should be typed first so that calculations can be made to enhance the presentation by inserting extra spaces, asterisks or a tailpiece on the shorter side.

Back page

Any wording on this page will contain matter of less importance; nevertheless, it should be displayed attractively.

Footnotes

1 Footnotes are used

1.1 To identify a reference or person quoted in the body of a report.
1.2 To give the source of a quotation cited in a report.
1.3 For explanations that may help or interest a reader.

2 Each footnote is

2.1 Preceded by the reference mark which corresponds to the reference in the text.
2.2 Typed in single spacing.

The reference mark in the text must be a superscript. In the footnote it is typed either on the same line or as a superscript. In the text **no** space is left between the reference mark and the previous character. In the footnote **one space** is left between the reference mark and the first word. The reference mark may be a number, asterisk, dagger or double dagger, and is placed outside the quotation mark and the punctuation mark.

It is now more popular to use one asterisk for the first footnote, two for the second and three for the third, rather than a dagger or double dagger, as the daggers are not always easy to construct on an electronic keyboard. The use of figures (in brackets) as a reference mark is favoured by printers.

In ordinary typewritten work, the footnote is usually placed at the foot of the page on which the corresponding reference appears in the body, and typed in **single** spacing. Care must be taken to leave enough space at the bottom of the page for the footnote, and, if a continuation page is needed, a clear space of 25 mm (1 inch) should be left after the last line of the footnote. It is usually separated from the main text by a horizontal line from margin to margin, and this line is typed by the underscore one single space after the last line of the text, and the footnote on the second single space below the horizontal line. If there is more than one footnote,

Exercise 1

Type the following table on plain A4 paper.

EUROPEAN COLLABORATIVE PROJECTS *

Aircraft/ Helicopter/ Space Project	Partner Nations	European Co	Output	
			Partner Nations	Exports
Alpha Jet	France	Dassault	~~30~~ 8 175	150
	~~UK~~ W Germany	Dornier	~~38~~ 175	
EH101	Italy UK	European Helicopter Industries (EHI)	38 38	– –
Space	Austria, UK Switzerland W Germany Netherlands Denmark Ireland Spain Norway Italy Sweden France Belgium	European Space Agency		

Concorde	France UK	Aerospatiale British Aerospace	8 8	– –

* As at 31.12.89

2.2 From 50(41) tap in 7(6) and set a tab stop for the start of the items on the right half of the page.

3 Leave left and right margins of 1 inch clear which means the left margin will be set at 13(11) and a tab stop set at 89(73). To find the starting point for the money column at the far right of the page, backspace from 89(73) one for one in the longest line of the column.

4 All headings, on right and left sides, start on the same lines, including the £ signs.

5 Use double spacing between each item. If any item requires more than one line, type the item in single spacing, indenting two spaces for the second and subsequent lines.

6 The totals on both sides must be typed opposite each other on the same line. This may mean leaving a blank space on the shorter side, before inserting the total and the total lines.

7 The horizontal lines above and below the total itself are typed as explained on page 152.

8 Blocked or centred display may be used with open or full punctuation.

Balance sheets

The method of setting out balance sheets is the same as that already explained above, although in some instances two separate sheets are used, the heading of the balance sheet running right across the two sheets without a break—half being typed on the liabilities side and ending close to the right edge of the paper, and the other half typed on the assets side starting close to the left edge of the sheet.

The side containing the larger number of items should be typed first, and, before starting to type the second sheet, you should make a light pencil mark to show the precise point at which the heading is to be continued, to ensure that the two parts of the heading are in line with one another. Also mark lightly in pencil on the second sheet the line on which the £ sign appears, the line on which the first item is to be typed and the exact position for the total, so that the two sides may coincide exactly.

Vertical balance sheets

Decide on the margins. Set left and right margin.

From the right margin backspace one for one for the longest item in the money column and set a tab stop. Where an item runs on to two lines, it is usual to indent the second line two spaces. If there are two columns of figures, leave a minimum of three spaces between each column.

Fit (manuscript)

1 It is sometimes necessary to divide a long manuscript among several typists. If the manuscript is in chapter form, the division should be made at the end of a chapter. If, however, the matter is continuous, the division must be made in such a way that the last line of each typist's section comes to the bottom of a page, so that it may run on without a break to the start of the next typist's section. This is known as 'fit'.

2 When a manuscript is divided in this way, care must be taken to see that each typist adopts the same margins, style for headings, etc, and that the ribbons and typefaces on all machines match.

Flow charts

A flow chart is a graphical representation of the flow of work, movement of documents, sequence of events, etc. By using lines and (sometimes) standard symbols (circles, diamonds, boxes, etc) a clear picture of a progression of happenings can be followed more easily.

The layout of flow charts varies widely and the design will depend on the characteristics of the particular topic. The aim of the flow chart is to help one complete a specific task step by step, or to identify the way in which a specified job is completed. By studying a flow chart, one can very often eradicate bottlenecks and wasteful operations.

Lines can flow vertically or horizontally provided that they show through letters, numbers or arrowheads the movement of a sequence of activities. Broken lines (continuous hyphens) are used for any function other than progressive flow.

When a flow chart has to be typed, it is usual to employ rectangular boxes for each step.

Flow charts are the foundation of computer programming. A chart has to be prepared so that the machine will execute each step of a particular task in logical succession and does not move forward to the next step until the previous step has been verified.

Before starting to type a flow chart, careful planning is essential. The first problem is to decide on the size of paper—it is better to err on the large side and you may have to use the paper lengthwise. If necessary, type a rough draft quickly to see what the longest horizontal line will look like. Unless otherwise instructed, leave three character spaces between items and at least one clear vertical space. When typing horizontal lines for boxes, turn up once before and twice after, although more, or less, space may be left between items or boxes.

Folded leaflets

The display and format used when typing a folded leaflet will depend on the way in which the page is

Exercise 2

Type the following table on A4 paper.

APPENDIX I

Required Reductions in Revenue Expenditure

(emphasize heading)

Budget Head	Revenue Budget Details		
	Savings Required	Current Budget	% of Current Budget
	£000s	£000s	£000s
Training & Management Development	50	135	37.0$ (3)
Personnel Administration Costs	10	78	11.49
Rationalization of the Senior Management Team . . .	260	80	30.77
Reduced Building Repairs & Maintenance	100	~~2~~77 (6)	14.17
Reduced Caretaking/Cleaning/ Porterage	138	420	32.86
Departmental Revenue Budget Allocations	1510	40	
Reduced Publicity Expenditure (including Sponsorship)	15	92	
Abolition of Catering Subsidies	25	25	

(take these 3 sets of figures from Data Files, filename APPEN, page 102 ~~100~~)

(on second thoughts please switch these 2 columns)

(Please type in ascending order of % savings to the current budget. Rule up appropriately. Use leader dots – 1 dot, 3 spaces.)

Folding letters and documents

Always use an envelope of suitable size so that letters and documents are not folded more than is necessary. A document folded many times is difficult to read and looks untidy.

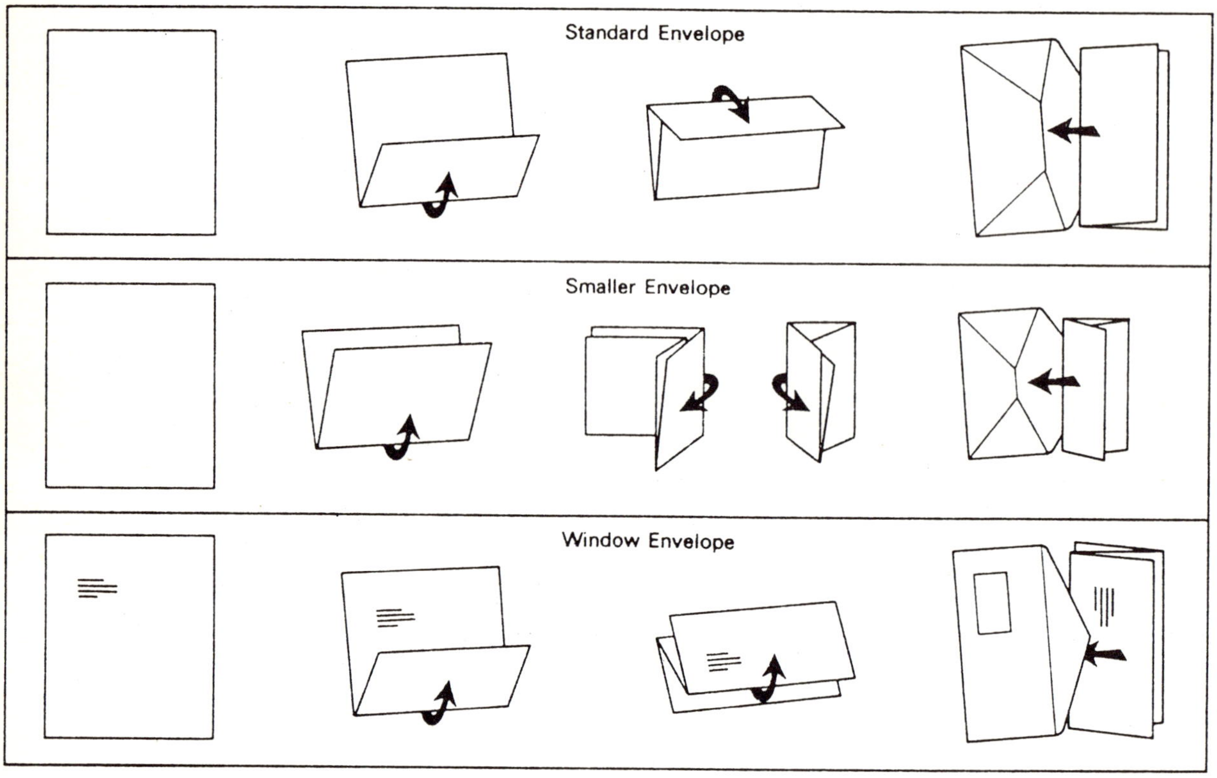

Errors

You will require individual remedial practice based on your needs; therefore, check your work carefully and make a note of the letters on which you made mistakes; then look in the index under **Drills** and choose the drill(s) that will help you overcome your faulty techniques.

Fair copy

Final copy typed on bond A4 paper in double spacing.

Fax

A FAX or facsimile machine is a copier that will transmit a document by electronic means usually over telephone lines from one location to another. At the distant end it appears as a printed copy, or facsimile, of the original. One of the great advantages of facsimile is the reduction of keyboarding errors because if the original copy is correctly prepared, no further typing or checking is necessary, and no carbon copies, envelopes, postage, etc, are required.

Figures in columns

Care must be taken to see that units come under units, tens under tens, etc. Where there are four or more figures, these are grouped in threes starting from the unit figure, a space being left, or a comma inserted, between each group.

Financial statements

There are certain accounts which you may be asked to type for your employer, such as balance sheet, income and expenditure account, receipts and payments account.

Guide to typing

1 The financial statement may be divided into two sides and may have a line down the middle of the page.

2 Leave the same number of spaces to the left and right of the centre of the page—say half an inch clear on either side.

   2.1 With A5 landscape paper or A4 paper, this would mean the centre of the paper is 50(41) and, to leave half an inch clear, backspace 7(6) from 50(41) plus the number of figures in the longest item in the figure column—set a tab stop for the start of the longest line in the left-hand figure column.

Exercise 3

Type the following table on plain A4 paper.

WINTHROP HUNT (CHARTERED ACCOUNTANTS)

SPECIALISERT ACCOUNTING COURSES – ~~JULY~~ JAN – JULY (typist add year)

Course Title	Content	Duration (Days)	Start Date
Intermediate Auditing & Accounting II	VAT; PAYE; more complex ~~auditing~~ procedures; unaudited accounts; materiality analytical review; ~~R~~ sample selection –	5	April 4 ~~Jun 14~~ (Type day before month please)
Personal Financial Planning	Life Assurance; pensions; investments; The Financial Services Act (1986)	2 (2 1-day modules	Feb 9 May 14 Jul 2
Insolvency II	Investigations; receiverships; distraints and execution; liquidator's duties; reservations of title	3	Jan 14 Mar 12
Share Valuation	Principles and purpose of share valuation; discounts; ~~S~~Share Valuation' Division; sources of info	1	(to be notified Sep)

(Switch these 2 columns)

Please note: Courses may be cancelled if insuff applications are rec'd opening bracket and one space after the final bracket.

Decimalized enumeration

In addition to the methods of enumeration explained above, it is modern practice to use the decimal point, followed by a figure, for subdivisions. For example, 4(a) and 4(b) would become 4.1 and 4.2; and 4(a) i and 4(a) ii would become 4.1.1 and 4.1.2. When using open punctuation, the decimal point for decimalized enumeration must be inserted. Leave two clear spaces after the final figure.

Envelopes

C5	162 × 229 mm ($6\frac{3}{8}$" × 9") takes A5 paper unfolded and A4 paper folded once
C6	114 × 162 mm ($4\frac{1}{2}$" × $6\frac{3}{8}$") takes A4 paper folded twice and A5 paper folded once
DL	110 × 220 mm ($4\frac{1}{4}$" × $8\frac{5}{8}$") takes A4 paper folded equally into three

Post Office regulations

1 Post Office regulations require the address to be parallel with the longest side of the envelope.
2 Postal town should be typed in capitals on a fresh line.
3 The postcode should be typed as follows:
  3.1 It is always the last item in the address and should have a line to itself.
  3.2 If it is impossible because of lack of space to put the code on a separate line, type it two to six spaces to the right of the last line.
  3.3 Always type the code in block capitals.
  3.4 Do not use full stops or any punctuation marks between or after the characters in the code.
  3.5 Leave **one** clear space between the two halves of the code.
  3.6 **Never** underline the code.

Example Open punctuation

Messrs W H Ramsay & Co
Mortimer Street
LONDON
W1N 8BA

Full punctuation

Messrs. W. H. Ramsay & Co.,
Mortimer Street,
LONDON.
W1N 8BA

Addressing envelopes, labels, postcards, etc (See also *Forms of address*, page 124.)

1 Always be sure to use an envelope sufficiently large to take the letter and any enclosure.
2 Many firms have their name and address printed in the top left corner. This ensures the safe and speedy return of the letter if, for any reason, it cannot be delivered.
3 Always type the envelope for each letter immediately after typing the letter.
4 Single spacing and blocked style are preferable on a small envelope. With larger envelopes the address may be better displayed and more easily read by being typed in double spacing.
5 On most envelopes the address should be started about one-third in from the left edge and the first line should be approximately half-way down.
6 Envelopes for overseas mail should have the town/city and country in upper case.
7 Special instructions.
  7.1 PERSONAL, CONFIDENTIAL, PRIVATE, URGENT should be typed in capitals, two spaces above the name of the addressee.
  7.2 FOR THE ATTENTION OF . . . is typed two spaces above the name and address of the addressee and may be in capitals or lower case with initial capitals when it must be underscored.
  7.3 RECORDED DELIVERY, REGISTERED MAIL and SPECIAL DELIVERY are typed in the top left corner in capitals, or immediately below the return address if there is one.
  7.4 FREEPOST and POSTE RESTANTE are typed after the name of the addressee.
  7.5 The words PAR AVION (BY AIRMAIL) are typed in the top left corner.
  7.6 Care of—typed c/o at the beginning of the line containing (a) the name or number of the house, eg Ms R Sharpe, c/o 21 Market Street, or (b) the name of the occupier, eg Ms R Sharpe, c/o Mrs U Needle, 21 Market Street.
  7.7 BY HAND is typed in the top right corner in capitals.
8 Remember to type the envelopes for any extra carbon copies which may be sent to the other offices or persons for their information.

Exercise 4

Type the following table on A4 paper. Keep columns 2 and 3 of an equal width.

Comments on Short listed Candidates {please make this heading part of the table}

Factor	Sheila Travers	Jon Gluzkowski
1. Physical Make-up	34, medium height well-dressed, speaks slowly & clearly	37, tall, fluent & positive in speech, smiles a lot
2. Attainments	12 yrs in telesales, then HND in Bus Studies; 3 yrs supervisory exp	Good degree (2i) + BPICS professional membership; Several yrs exp in mail order
3. General Intelligence	I wd estimate th both candidates are in the top 5%	
4. Special Aptitudes	Dealing w. customers & personal callers, ~~computers~~, figures work	Fluent French & Polish
5. Interests	Sports - squash, swimming, interiors, foreign travel	DiY enthusiast, fishing
6. Disposition	Immed likeable, {& I wd suggest} resp & trustworthy; high level of integrity	Somewhat abrasive on 1st meeting, but one warms to him. Highly ambitious.
7. Circumstances	Works locally, buying a house within commuting distance	Has a house to sell in London {which is already on the market}. ~~Recently~~ Just married.

Key in exercise 4 (filename SHORT) for 10-pitch printout. Use the save function for the first horizontal ruled line and copy where necessary; also, use the vertical line key for inserting vertical lines. When you have completed this task, save under filename SHORT. Retrieve the document and follow the instructions for text editing on page 100.

4 Internal memory—may be stored permanently on a read only memory chip or may be lost when the machine is switched off.
5 External memory—any storage medium (disk) that can be removed from the system.
6 Mailing applications.

Elision

This is the omission of a letter (usually a vowel) when pronouncing a word, eg wouldn't, can't, don't. This form of abbreviation should **not** be used in typescript unless you are quoting direct speech, ie using quotation marks, or instruction has been given to use it.

Ellipsis (omission of words)

Words are sometimes deliberately omitted at the beginning, end or in the middle of a sentence. Such omission is indicated by the use of three spaced full stops with a space either side, as follows: . . . .
When quotation marks come before the ellipsis, there is a space between the mark and the first full stop. There is also a space before the final quotation mark, eg " . . . ".

Embolden

An electronic machine may have a **bold** function key. Usually, this key is depressed before typing the chosen word(s) which will then appear in a much darker print and thus be more emphatic.

Emphasis

See ***Effective display***, page 117.

Endorsements

See ***Legal documents***, page 128.

Enumeration

An enumeration is a set of numbered/lettered paragraphs or lines that may be displayed in several different ways.

1 The numbers may project to the left of the first line of the paragraph, with the second and subsequent lines blocked underneath the first line of the paragraph—as in this paragraph. Punctuation must not be inserted after a number when typing in open punctuation—leave two clear spaces. Also, leave two spaces after the full stop when full punctuation is used. Indented or hanging paragraphs may be used.
2 In some cases the numbers are put in brackets, eg (2) in which case two spaces are left and no full stop is inserted after the final bracket.
3 Letters may be used in place of numbers.
4 Where there are subdivisions of enumerated items, these can be distinguished in order of importance as follows:
4.1 Capital roman numerals for main division.
4.2 Upper case letters for first subdivision.
4.3 Arabic numbers, small letters or small roman numerals for further subdivisions.
5 There must be a clear linespace above, below and between lettered/numbered items.

NOTE: In business, you will find that in order to save space, your employer may prefer you to leave no space **between** the lettered/numbered items.

6 When roman numerals are used in enumerations, these may be blocked on the left or right. Do not insert full stops when using open punctuation.

Left—example with full punctuation.

I. Two spaces should be left after the full stop following the **longest** numeral.
II. Therefore, there will be four spaces after I, three spaces after II, two spaces after III and
III. three spaces after IV.
IV.

Right—example with open punctuation.

I Two spaces should be left after the numeral. It
II will be necessary to indent two spaces before typing I, one space before II, no space before
III III, and one space before IV.
IV

NOTES: (a) The punctuation before the start of an enumeration may be a full stop, a colon (most popular); a colon and dash (:-) which is considered old-fashioned; a dash (space before the hyphen).
(b) The punctuation at the end of each enumeration could be no punctuation at all, a comma, a semi-colon, or a full stop, depending on the sense. The final item in a list would normally have a full stop. Always follow instructions, the copy or the house style. **Be consistent!**

Continuous prose

When using enumerations in continuous prose where the items 'run on' (are not listed underneath each other), the numbers or letters should be enclosed in brackets. There is one space before the

Exercise 5

Prepare and type the table from the details below.

Events in chronological order please.

DIARY OF EVENTS JANUARY/FEBRUARY ← use this heading - add yr.

9-12 Feb, New Systems, Brighton, Organizers - Graeme Morton, 45 The Quadrant, Brighton, BN2 1RT (0273) 55002

3-6 Feb, The TV Show, Frankfurt, Organizers - Spectrum Conferences, 75 New Lincoln St, London, SE1 2YT (01-356-9442)

10-13 Jan, The Retail Show, New York, Organizers - NRMP, 300 West Avenue, New York, NY10004, USA (010 1-212 6688)

19-22 Jan, What's New in Automation? The Barbican, Organizers - Creed Trade Fairs, 15 Bedford Sq, London, WC1P 9VN (01-593-9264)

12-15 Feb, Comtech North, GMEX Centre, Manchester, Organizers - (as for New Systems)

Date	Event	Location	Organizers

(name + tel no only)

Exercise 6

Prepare and type the table from the details below.

Please schedule at ½-hourly intervals beginning at 9.30am. Alphabetical order, but where a candidate has to travel - please put them as late as poss.

John W Dawson 8 Charlotte St Macclesfield
SK11 6EF (0625) 692301
Winston Brown 15 Broad Lane Terr Deeside Clwyd
CH5 2NW (0244) 79475
Suzanne Lander 51-67 Fitzroy Avenue Belfast BT7 1HT
(0232) 482810
Georgina Barber Flat 4 135 Bristol Rd Selly Oak
Birmingham B29 6DH 021-471-55882
Jane Taylor 559 Wolverhampton Rd South Birmingham
B32 2AY 021-420-36666
Daljit Seehra 54b Bournville Rd Bournville Birmingham
B30 3LP 021-458-66916

Please type this heading in lower case with initial caps.

INTERVIEW SCHEDULE FOR TRAINEE BUYER		
Time	Name	Tel No
use 24hr clock		

TYLER & MASON PRODUCTS LTD, BIRMINGHAM

addresses of the customers and the filename of the form letter to be typed.

Standard paragraphs are also keyed in and stored. The author will supply the names and addresses and, on instruction, the machine will retrieve and assemble the paragraphs into a letter. In some cases there may be additions or deletions.

Often-used forms are also stored and are retrieved and completed as and when required.

The electronic keyboard and the VDU have made production of repetitive text very much easier and time-saving. Any variables can be inserted quickly and easily (there is no difficulty with alignment when you have a VDU) and the complete document printed out as an original—as distinct from a duplicated or printed document with the variables added.

Document presentation

See page viii.

Double underscore

See ***Totals***, page 152.

Draft

If your employer asks you to type a draft copy of a document, it would be wise for you to enquire whether the document is likely to be radically revised or whether the draft is to show how the document will look when completed.

If the document is likely to be extensively revised after typing, then the draft should be in double or treble spacing with wide margins. On the other hand, if the draft is to show how it will look when finished, then it should be typed in the style required for the finished job.

The word DRAFT should always be typed in capitals at the top left-hand margin at least one clear space above the start of the document.

Dropped head

See ***Chapter headings***, page 112.

Duplicating process

See ***Reprography***, page 140.

Effective display and emphasis

Matter can be effectively and artistically displayed if **emphasis** is given to important lines by the judicial use of:

1 Spaced capitals (one space between each letter and three spaces between each word).
2 Closed capitals (one or two spaces between each word).
3 Underlining of certain words or lines.
4 Initial capitals and small letters with or without underlining.
5 Insetting of lines or items from the left margin or left and right margins.
6 Bold type if this function is available on your electronic machine.
7 Hanging paragraphs.
8 Changing the linespacing.

NOTE: Care must be taken not to overdo any one of these methods; otherwise, no line will stand out more prominently than another, thus detracting from the general appearance.

Preparing a layout of a notice

Before typing an unarranged notice or tabulation, or when rearranging a table, etc, prepare a 'layout', ie a rough plan in pencil, showing the best arrangement of the matter and the number of lines required. Keep the layout before you as you type. Where the display or rearrangement is complicated, it is a good plan to type a rough copy of the longest line and/or parts that are not clear.

Electronic typewriters

While the electric typewriter consists of mechanical parts and electrical wiring, the electronic typewriter has silicon chips to decode the keyboard instructions and operate the editing and storage functions.

On electronic typewriters the printing element is a daisywheel, with the exception of the older IBM machines where the golf ball head is still used.

The following are some of the facilities to be found on electronic typewriters:

1 Automatic—carriage return, underscoring, bold face, vertical ruling, margin sets and additional margin sets, horizontal centring, reverse tabulation, decimal tabulation, justification of right margin, etc.
2 'Window' display—the typist can read the text line by line before printing it. While the words are in display, the typist can make corrections, add or take away words, etc.
3 10, 12 and 15 pitch plus proportional spacing.

SKILL BUILDING 6

1 *Alphabetic sentences*

Type each sentence twice.

Professional double glazing is likely to raise the value of the bungalow much more quickly than a major extension.

Everyone enjoyed walking and shopping in the busy plaza for inexpensive, but good quality souvenirs to carry home.

2 *Practise making handwritten insertions*

rôle   provençale   Zoë   resumé   à la carte   table d'hôte

4 ℓ (4 litres)   ↑   ↓   ←   →   ↔   «   »   ∵   ∴

3 *Improve control of words with common prefixes*

offer official office offside offset officer offence officious offend offhand

manager manageress management manageable managerial managing manage

paper paperwork paperback paperweight paperclip paperknife

pass passing passable passbook password passage passport passenger

overdraft overcome overdue overhead overlap overlook overseas overtime

superb supervise supersede supertax supermarket superior superficial

subconscious subdue subcontract subject subheading submission submerge

4 *Production development from manuscript*

Reading time: 1 minute   Target typing time: 2 minutes

PUBLIC RELATIONS EXECUTIVE (TEMP MATERNITY COVER)
Grant Archer is a (wholly owned) subsidiary of Grant Howarth
& Associates, an org specializing in the provision
of financial services to (UK) bus in the. At our
Group Head Office in the West End we are ~~now~~
looking for a PR specialist to join a small
professional team on a temp basis (from Jan to July) of next yr.
The main area of work wl be assisting w
arrangements for exhibitions & other (major) PR
events.

500 keystrokes (100 words)

always appear at the set scale point and the figures will be in alignment (units under units, tens under tens, etc) before and after the decimal point.

Degree sign

If the typewriter does not have a special key for the degree sign, it is represented by the small o raised half a space. When typing 20 degrees, type 20° with no space between the figures and the degree sign; but when typing 20 degrees Fahrenheit or 20 degrees Celsius, type 20 °F or 20 °C—note that there is a space between the figures and the degree sign, but no space between the degree sign and the F or C.

Deliberate errors

Certain exercises, both in this textbook and in some examinations, contain deliberate errors of spelling, punctuation and relationship between subject and verb. These errors may or may not be indicated by encircling the incorrect word(s). Your knowledge of the use of words, spelling, etc, should be such that you notice and correct the errors when typing. As a typist in business you will be expected to correct any spelling errors accidentally made by the author.

Diagrams

See ***Allocating space***, page 106.

Display

1 Horizontal

1.1 **Block-centred** Centre the longest line which gives the starting point for all lines.
1.2 **Centred** All lines centred on the paper or on the typing line. To find the centre point of the typing line, add together the points at which the margins are set and divide by two.

2 Vertical

2.1 Find the number of vertical lines on the paper being used.
2.2 Count the number of lines and blank spaces between the lines, in the exercise to be typed.
2.3 Deduct 2.2 from 2.1 and divide by two (ignore fractions).
2.4 Turn up the number of linespaces arrived at in 2.3 **plus one extra**.

See also ***Effective display and emphasis***, page 117.

Distractions

See page 25.

Distribution lists

See ***Business letters, 4.15***, page 110.
Instead of typing cc followed by the names of the persons to whom copies of a document should be sent, your boss may require you to type a distribution/circulation list. Examples are given on pages 5 and 7.

Ditto marks

When the same word is repeated in consecutive lines of display matter, double quotation marks may be used under the repeated word. If there is more than one word repeated, the quotation marks must be typed under each word. The abbreviation 'do' (with the full stop in full punctuation) may be used under a group of words. When used with blocked style, the ditto marks should be blocked at the beginning of each word; with centred style, the ditto marks should be centred under the word(s).

Division of words

See ***Line-end division***, page 129.

Document assembly

In word processing terms, this is known as boilerplating. Many documents that businesses use will contain similar information and wording and, in order to save time, form or skeleton letters containing the **constant** (unchanging) information are prepared, keyed in and stored. Space will be left for the date, inside address, salutation and any other **variables**.

Each form letter is given a filename so that it can be retrieved easily, and a special code is placed at each point so that the machine will stop and the relevant information can be inserted at the position of the cursor. If the same letter is being sent to a number of customers, the typist keys in the names and addresses, and command keys are used to merge the two banks of information. Each customer will then receive an individually addressed and typed letter. Also, the machine, when instructed, will automatically type the name and address on a label or an envelope.

The author does not have to dictate the letter, she or he simply supplies the typist with the names and

Exercise 1

Type the following job description on A4 plain paper. Rule as indicated.

JOB DESCRIPTION } centre each line

GORING DISTRICT COUNCIL }

JOB TITLE: TYPIST/CLERICAL ASSISTANT | Grade: II/III

Salary: £5K - £7,300

BASIC ROLE:

[inset by 5 spaces] To provide a sec support service for the Org & Methods Group on a part-time basis.

MAIN DUTIES & resp: (please number the following points 1-9)

The typing of memos, often of a technical nature, from manuscript, audio & shorthand dictation. [letters, reports & forms]

WP (training ~~wl be~~ given on our equipment).

Telephone work - (i) dealing with queries from internal staff;

(ii) Assisting in obtaining prices of new equipment from suppliers;

(iii) obtaining info from a variety of ref sources.

[type WP and O & M in full throughout]

Photocopying as required

Keeping The Head of Org and Methods diary

Making appts

Servicing the O & M users Cttee

Setting up & maintaining a group filing system

Other duties as required from time to time by the Head of the O & M Group.

WORKING ARRANGEMENTS:

The successful applicant wl be expected to work 9 a.m. to 1300 hrs, Mon to Fri

TO WHOM RESP: Head of the O & M Group

training. He or she will want to know what academic qualifications you have, what specialist qualifications you have, what your main interests are, what recreational activities and hobbies you have, etc. Sometimes this information is referred to as a personal data sheet or a curriculum vitae.

No two people are alike and no two personal data sheets should be exactly the same. It is possible that you will arrange your personal record of your career in a somewhat different way when applying for different jobs. You will always wish to emphasize the qualities and qualifications that would make you valuable in the particular job for which you are applying.

If you have worked—for a salary or as a volunteer—you should mention this. Your work need not have been closely related to the work for which you are applying, but it may indicate to your prospective employer a measure of your intelligent thinking, dependability, resourcefulness, etc. Always list temporary or part-time work (holidays and Saturdays only).

It is usual to include the name and address of one referee. See that you give the person's name—correctly spelt—his/her title (Mr/Mrs/Miss/Ms) and correct address and telephone number. **Never**, in any circumstances, give as a reference a person whose permission you have not asked in advance.

Your curriculum vitae/personal data sheet must be perfectly typed and clearly displayed with main, sub, and side/shoulder headings. The following points should be covered: your name and address; date of birth; secondary education/college/university; secretarial/office training; examinations passed; work experience (if any); special interests; name and address of a referee; date on which you are available for employment.

Cursor

When a visual display unit is used in conjunction with an electronic machine, the typing appears on the VDU screen. On the screen there is a movable dot (hyphen) which indicates the typing point at which the next typed character will appear. This movable dot/hyphen is called the cursor.

Data files

As well as being an expert typist, it is essential for you to have practice in finding and using information from various sources. Throughout this textbook, there are exercises where it is necessary for you to refer to another part of the book, or to the **data files**, for data to enable you to complete an exercise. The **data files** are on pages 102–103.

Dead keys

Some typewriters are provided with keys which, when depressed, do not cause the carriage/carrier to move forward the usual single character space. These are known as 'dead keys'. They are usually fitted for foreign accents so that the accent can be struck first and, without the necessity of backspacing, the letter key is then struck.

Electronic machines may have a few dead keys, eg a key for inserting vertical lines. Refer to the manufacturer's handbook for further details.

Decimals

1 Always use full stop for decimal point.

2 Leave **no** space before or after decimal point.

3 No punctuation is required at end of figures, except at the end of a sentence.

Decimals in columns

1 When typing decimal figures in columns, see that the decimal points come under one another.
2 There must be the same number of decimal places in each line of the column, so that where necessary the figure 0 is used to make up the required number of decimal places. For example, if there are two decimal places, type 6.00, 6.60, 6.66. If three decimal places, type 6.000, 6.600, 6.660, etc. If there is no whole number, type 0 before the decimal point, eg 0.66.
3 If pounds and pence are typed in columns, the £ sign is typed over the unit figure of the pounds. No sign appears over the pence or decimals of a pound.
4 If the column contains whole pounds only, the £ sign is centred over the longest item, eg:

£
240

5 With blocked display, the £ sign is typed over the first figure of the longest line, or over the £ sign if one is used before the total.

Decimal tabulation

On electronic machines the decimal tabulation function enables the typist to set a tab stop for the decimal point. No matter how many figures there are before and after the decimal tab stop, the point will

Exercise 2

Type the following press release on A4 plain paper in double spacing. Leave 10 lines clear at the top of the page. Press releases are explained on pages 135–136.

PRESS RELEASE [Not for publication before 12 noon on 14 Mar

CAPS

(Grant Systems) PL&C announce a revolution in [small] bus computing w the launch of their [new] OS/2 compatible ~~a~~ microcomputer. (insert 1)

This exciting new high-performance system offers a colour monitor, mouse, 20 Mb hard disk, EGA graphics adaptor, & a quality laser printer (insert 2) at a special introductory price of [only] £999.00. [Accompanying this hardware is a fully-integrated software package ~~wh combines~~ combining a powerful word processor w diary, spreadsheet & database facilities.)

Easy-to-use desktop publishing software wl also be ~~made~~ available for a modest £99.00. (insert 3)

Marketing Director Keith Grant says [' We are now the leading UK mfr in small bus IT, & the only co offering a quality system in this price bracket - our products represent a major breakthrough in the microcomputer market') single spacing for this quote, inset by 5 spaces

G—— S—— PLC has again come up w an innovative system at a price wh the ~~customer~~ ~~consumer~~ can afford. The co has doubled ~~its~~ profits since 1988, & this yr promises to be the most successful yet, w record sales in the UK. [For further info contact (typist - take from Data Files, filename STAND Sp3, page 103)

ENDS

(The '1992' is available thro' selected [electronics] stores throughout the UK from early May; potential dealers shd contact Bryan Lewis on (0203) 44013 direct / the launch wl be supported by an extensive television & poster advertising campaign)

(1) ~~the~~ the '1992'

(2) (wh has an outturn of 5 A4 pages per min)

(3) The novice user wl quickly master the system using our new high-speed training package.

(PRESS RELEASE & ENDS IN SPACED CAPS PLEASE)

Key in exercise 2 (filename PRESS) for 12-pitch printout. Embolden main heading and the word ENDS; use automatic underline key for subheading and justify right margin. When you have completed this task, save under filename PRESS. Retrieve the document and follow the instructions for text editing on page 100.

Continuation sheets

See ***Business letters*, *4.17*,** page 110.

Continuous stationery

Invoice sets are usually in continuous form with perforations between the sets which may be NCR (no carbons required) paper or one-time only carbon paper. Paper for word processing printouts may also be in continuous form edged by sprocket holes for use on the tractor-feed device. The paper may be letterheads, invoice forms, payslips, etc.

Copy

To distinguish the copy of a document from an original, type the word COPY at the top, and the word (SIGNED) (in brackets) before the signatory's name (if typed).

Correction of errors

Correct the error as soon as you know you have made a mistake and read through the whole exercise when you have finished typing it and while the paper is still in the machine, in case there is an error you had not noticed before.

There are various methods which may be used to correct errors:

1 Rubber

1.1 Turn up the paper so that the error is on top of the platen or paper table.
1.2 Press the paper tightly against the cylinder or paper table to prevent slipping.
1.3 Erase the error by rubbing gently up and down, blowing away rubber dust as you do so. (Too much pressure may cause a hole.)
1.4 If you are using a new or heavily inked ribbon, erase first with a soft rubber and then with a typewriter eraser.
1.5 Turn paper back to writing line and insert correct letter or letters.
1.6 Always use a clean rubber.

NOTE: If the typewriter has a carriage, move it to the extreme right or left to prevent rubber dust from falling into the mechanism of the machine.

2 Correction paper

These specially coated strips of paper are placed in front of the printing point over the error on the original and between the carbon paper(s) and the copy sheet(s). The incorrect character(s) is (are) typed again through the correction paper(s) which will cover up or lift off the incorrect character(s). Remove the coated strips and type the correct character(s).

3 Correction fluid

Correction fluid is produced in various shades to match the typing paper and is applied with a small brush. The incorrect letter is obliterated and when the fluid is dry, the correct letter may be typed over the top. The liquid may be spirit- or water-based. If the spirit-based liquid is used, it is necessary to add thinner to the bottle as, after a time, the original liquid tends to thicken. Spirit-based liquid dries more quickly than water-based. Avoid unsightly blobs. Use tissue paper to wipe the brush.

4 Correction ribbon

Some electric typewriters and most electronic typewriters are fitted with a correction ribbon. When making a correction with a correction ribbon, it is necessary to:

4.1 Backspace to the error.
4.2 Press the correction key—the error is then removed.
4.3 Type the correct letter(s).

5 Correction on electronic typewriters

Electronic typewriters are equipped with a memory and may have a thin window display so that automatic corrections can be made—from a few characters to ten or more lines. The correction is made by backspacing the delete key and then typing in the correct character(s). Electronic typewriters may be fitted with a relocate key which, when depressed, returns the carrier to the last character typed before the correction was made.

NOTE: The latest electronic typewriters have visual display units and corrections are made by use of the automatic overstrike, delete or erase functions. They also have a disk drive and diskettes.

6 Corrections on word processors/ computers

To make a correction on a word processor/computer, one would use the automatic overstrike, delete or erase functions.

Curriculum vitae: a brief account of one's career

When you apply for a job, your prospective employer will require a summary of your education and

Exercise 3

Type the following chairman's statement on plain A4 paper in single spacing.

(indent paragraphs)

DENES ~~Y~~F ASHIONS PLC - CHAIRMAN'S STATEMENT

1 (Review of the Yr) ← Emphasize all these headings

Altho' we reported an outstanding yr in 19~~89~~90, difficult trading conditions ~~has~~ we meant only a marginal 2% increase in sales this yr (almost wholly confined to the 15-22 age range. (Coupled w an absense of strong fashion trends)

The fashion market is projected to grow @ 4% annually over the next 5 yrs & our primary goal must be to ~~increase~~ improve our market share.

To resume our growth path we must suceed in capturing a larger share of the lucrative 25-30 yr old market.

2 Identifying New Customers

A re-think on in-store changing room accomodation in line w our competitors is vital. We are already making better use of wall space to display merchandise, to guide customers to the right sections within stores & (to spell out fashion statements)

For next yr we intent to improve shop layout further and reduce congestion by carrying slightly lower levels of stocks, improving walkways & introducing new fixtures to display more clothing to better advantage. Our "customer care" training programme will be extended to cover all employees. The trend towards catering for a more affluent older population wl require improvements in garment quality, & a consequent increase in the average price of clothing items. Currently, our designers are giving attention to the "career dressing" market w mix ~~un~~ & match seps, colour-coordinated ranges & a wider choice of suits & tailored jackets.

3 Growth in Retail Outlets

During the yr we have opened 10 new outlets in Chichester, Exeter, Great Yarmouth, Bradford & Milton Keynes.

2" (51mm)

please draw this box on the right-hand side of the page opposite point 2

3" (76mm)

(Type ~~B~~ DRAFT in top r-h corner please)

clients. The original is usually typed on a master sheet (stencil or offset litho) and a quantity is 'run off'.

Where individually typed circular letters are required, they may be prepared on a word processor or electronic typewriter and then printed.

1 Reference

In usual position.

2 Date

Typed in various ways, eg:
21 October 1990
October 1990 (month and year only)
Date as postmark. (These words are typed where you normally type the date.)

3 Name and address of addressee

3.1 Space may be left for this, and in that case the details are typed on individual sheets after they have been 'run off'. When preparing the master (or draft), turn up eight single spaces after the date (leaving seven clear) before typing the salutation.

3.2 Very often the name and address of addressee are not inserted and, if this is so, no space need be left when the master is prepared. Turn up two single spaces after the date.

4 Salutation

4.1 Dear   , the remainder of the salutation is typed in when the name and address are inserted.

4.2 Dear Sir, Dear Madam, Dear Sir(s), Dear Sir/Madam. See 'Deletions' opposite.

5 Signature

The person writing the letter may or may not sign it. If the writer is signing, type the complimentary close, etc, in the usual way. If the writer is not signing, type Yours faithfully and company's name* in the usual position, turn up two single spaces and type the name of the person writing the letter, then turn up two spaces and type the designation.

* If the company's name is not being inserted, turn up two single spaces after Yours faithfully and type the name of the writer, then turn up two spaces and type the writer's designation.

6 Tear-off portion

Sometimes a letter or circular will have a tear-off portion at the foot so that a customer may fill in certain details and return the tear-off portion to the sender.

The minimum space to be left after the complimentary close or signatory is one clear space. In other words, turn up a minimum of two spaces and then type from **edge to edge** of the paper **continuous dots** or **continuous hyphens**, then turn up two spaces and type the information on the tear-off portion.

Where blank spaces are left for details to be filled in, use **continuous dots** (or the **underscore**) and **double spacing**. Remember to leave one clear space after the last character typed before starting the dots or underscore and one clear space at the end of the dots or underscore before the next typed character if there is one, eg:

(space) (space)
Surname . . . . Forename(s) . . . .

The exception to this is when the dotted line (or underscore) follows the sterling sign, eg £________, and if the first letter of the courtesy title has been typed, eg M______. Of course, the first figure must be typed close to the £ sign, and the first letter close to the M.

7 Deletions

It is often necessary to delete letters or words in a form or circular letter. For instance, a circular letter may start **Dear Sir/Madam** and if the letter is being sent to a lady, the word **Sir/** would be deleted. To delete previously typed characters such as the foregoing, use an X aligned precisely with the characters already typed.

8 Ruled or dotted lines

In some form letters and forms you may have to type on ruled or dotted lines. You must type slightly above the line so that none of the descending characters touches the line. For example:

going   going

Clean and uncreased work

Typed work that is accurate and quickly produced can be spoilt by dirty finger marks, smudges and, particularly on the carbon copy, creases. It is important to be organized and methodical. Keep your workstation neat and tidy with everything within easy reach; this will aid you in producing neat and clean documents.

Combination characters

See ***Special signs, symbols and marks***, page 143.

Figure A shows a picture of our new ~~HK~~ ~~Exeter~~ store. (Acton Keynes)

4 To Sum Up

This yr 5.25 m women aged 18-39 have visited our stores & spent a massive £45m ~~between them~~

Denes are still ~~UK's~~ Britain's No 1 specialist in mainstream women's fashion, & management feel confident th the co has a bright future ahead of it.

(plse change double quotes to single quotes throughout)

Key in exercise 3 (filename CHAIR) for 15-pitch printout. Embolden the numbered shoulder headings, and use the indent function/indent tab setting for the indented paragraphs. When you have completed this task, save under filename CHAIR. Retrieve the document and follow the instructions for text editing on page 100.

Exercise 4

Type the following notice of meeting on A4 plain paper.

NOTICE OF MEETING ← (spaced caps)

Notice is hereby given that the 22nd (use words) Annual General Meeting of F V Booth Plc wl be held ~~in the~~ (at) Strand House, London SW1P 4RA on Wed 29 Aug 1990 at 11 am for the following purposes:

Resolution 1 To receive the reports of the Directors and the financial statements.

Resolution 2 To declare a final dividend on the ordinary shares.

(use shoulder headings for Resolution 1, 2, etc)

Resolution 3 To re-elect the following directors: (uc. d)

Mr J W Gilder (Resolution 3a)
Sir William Field (Resolution 3b) (indent)

Resolution 4 To reappoint the auditors and to authorize the Board of Directors to fix their remuneration.

Resolution 5 To transact any other ordinary business of the meeting.

By order of the Board (uc. o)
Graham P Francis
Secretary

Strand House, London SW1P 4RA → (align address at right margin)

6.4 **Letters to the United Kingdom**
Ms A Halcrow
12 Scotland Avenue
PENRITH
Cumbria
GREAT BRITAIN
CA11 7AA

NOTE: For overseas mail, the name of the **town** and the name of the **country** should be in capitals.

Carbon paper

Light-weight carbon paper produces the sharpest impressions and can be used for between five and seven copies. Medium-weight carbon paper is most commonly used for making three or four copies. Carbon film has a plastic backing instead of a paper backing and is therefore more durable. The following factors need to be considered when choosing carbon paper:

1 The size of the typeface: 10 pitch will give a much clearer impression than, say, 15 pitch.
2 The condition of the typewriter and whether it is manual or electric.
3 The weight of the letterhead sheets and second sheet.
4 The number of carbon copies usually made.

Usually the top right- or left-hand corner of carbon paper is cut away and you should, when taking a number of carbon copies (manifolding), always place the carbon paper so that the cut-off corners are together. When the typing has been completed, hold the pages above the cut-off corners and the carbons will drop on to the desk.

Some organizations use different coloured paper for different departments so that copies are instantly recognizable. For example, white copies for sales department, yellow copies for works manager, green copies for company secretary, etc.

Cards

The typist will have to type cards for a variety of purposes such as a mailing list, telephone index, credit sales index, etc.

When cards are to be filed in alphabetical order, then the filing 'word' must start near the top edge of the card, say, half an inch down. Other information on the card should be suitably displayed with at least 13 mm ($\frac{1}{2}$ inch) margins all round, unless the contents are such that it is not possible to leave margins.

A fair amount of practice in typing cards is essential and a great deal of care is necessary in order to see that the card does not slip, or become out of alignment, when turned up/down. A backing sheet will help; otherwise, fold over about 13 mm/25 mm ($\frac{1}{2}$ inch/1 inch) at the top of a sheet of A4 paper, place the card underneath the fold and feed into the machine.

Catchword

In memos and other documents a catchword is sometimes used. When a continuation sheet is necessary, the first word or two of the text appearing on the continuation sheet is sometimes typed at the foot of the preceding page below the last line and aligned at the right margin. CONTINUED or PTO may be used instead of the catchword, but not the number of the next page.

Chairman's agenda

The chairman's agenda may contain more information than the agenda for the other committee members. The right side of a chairman's agenda may be left blank, so that he can write in the decisions reached on the various points. The word **notes** may be typed (either centred or blocked) on the right side and the items re-numbered at the centre of the typing line. Open or full punctuation may be used.

Chapter headings and chapter numbers

Leave 25 mm (1 inch) clear at the top of the page before typing the chapter number. Alternatively, you may use a 'dropped head', ie the chapter number is typed 51 mm (2 inches) to 76 mm (3 inches) from the top edge of the paper in roman numerals or arabic numbers. The heading is typed in capital letters two single spaces below the chapter number. The chapter number and heading may be centred on the typing line or blocked at the left margin.

Circular letters

Circulars, or circular letters, are letters of same contents which are sent to a number of customers or

Exercise 5

Type the following references on A5 landscape paper. Where items are underscored, you may use either italics or underscore.

REFS

1 J Burton 'Going for Gold' The Reviewer Mar/Apr 1989.

5 ~~2~~ See The Times 6 Apr 1988 & the Guardian 14 Jun '88 & contrary view by PD James 'Getting the 1980s into Perspective' Quarterly Banking Review May 1990.

2 Challenge: Is It Still Here? Graham Parker (Ed) Haldon Press (1989).

3 Survival of the Fittest House of Commons 311 (1990).

4 F McEvoy & M Magus 'Shaping up to a New Bus Future' in McEvoy Magus Dawkins & Witley (Eds) The Enterprise Culture Roger Willow (1990).

Exercise 6

Type the following agenda on A4 plain paper, following the display given on page 105.

Meeting of the Info Technology Planning Group to be held in Room VH49, Waites Building on Mon (second Mon of next mth - typist please insert date) at 1100 hrs. (underline heading)

A G E N D A

1. Apologies for absense
2. Minutes of the previous meeting (second Wed of last mth - please add date)
3 Matters arising from the minutes
6 ~~4~~ Report on the Personal Departments pilot w expert systems
5 Central budgetary allocations for Apr (add yr)
4 ~~6~~ Renewal of maintenance contract ~~w.~~ from Willis Systems Ltd

(Take items 7 & 8 from Data Files, filename AGEN, page 102)

continuation sheet, and sometimes the name or initials of the sender are printed in the top left corner. Otherwise, always use a plain sheet of the same size, colour and quality as the previous page. The only details which you should type are the following: name of addressee, page number and date, starting on the fourth single line from the top. In fully-blocked letters, all these details are typed at the left margin in double spacing, in the following order: page number, date, name of addressee. In indented letters, the name of the addressee is typed at the left margin, the page number is centred in the typing line, and the date ends at the right margin. The letter is continued on the third single space below the continuation sheet details.

When a continuation sheet is needed, the letter must be so arranged that at least three or four lines are carried to the second page. On no account must the continuation sheet contain only the complimentary close and name of writer. Also, at least two lines of a paragraph should be left at the bottom of the first page. Do not divide a word from one page to the next.

If the reverse of the paper is used for the continuation sheet, then the margins must also be reversed, eg first sheet: left margin 38 mm ($1\frac{1}{2}$ inches), right margin 25 mm (1 inch); continuation sheet: left margin 25 mm (1 inch), right margin 38 mm ($1\frac{1}{2}$ inches).

NOTE: The word 'CONTINUED' or 'PTO' is seldom used in letters. A catchword is sometimes used, ie the first word of the text appearing on a continuation sheet is typed at the foot of the preceding page. The number of the next page must not be used as a catchword.

4.18 **Signing letters on behalf of the writer**

4.18.1 Your employer may ask you to type and sign a letter on his behalf. The complimentary close in this case would be:

Yours faithfully
J R BLACK & CO LTD
Helen M. Grant
John Black
Director

or

Yours faithfully,
J. R. BLACK & CO. LTD.
Helen M. Grant
Dictated by Mr. Black
and signed in his absence

4.18.2 Your employer may ask you to write a letter on his behalf and sign it, or circumstances may necessitate your writing on behalf of your employer, eg 'Mr Black has asked me to thank you for your letter dated 21 June, etc'. The complimentary close would be:

Yours faithfully
J R BLACK & CO LTD
Helen M. Grant
Helen M Grant (Mrs)
Secretary to J Black, Director

or

Yours sincerely,
Helen M. Grant
Mrs. Helen M. Grant
Secretary to J. Black, Director

4.19 **Titled persons** The less formal wording is now generally used, eg the salutation: Dear Lord Newton; complimentary close: I am, Sir, Yours sincerely/respectfully/faithfully, etc.

5 Folding letters

Letters and documents should be neatly folded to fit the particular size of envelope used. It is important to make sure that the envelope is of a suitable size for any enclosures that may be included.

6 Overseas mail

6.1 **Airmail—countries outside Europe** In the letter, the word AIRMAIL is typed two single spaces after the last line of the reference or the date if the date is typed at the left margin. On the envelope the words PAR AVION (BY AIRMAIL) are typed in the top left corner, eg:

PAR AVION (BY AIRMAIL)

Mr J de Munck
88–86 West Street
Elmhurst
NEW YORK
NY 11373
UNITED STATES OF AMERICA

6.2 **The All-up European Service** Letters (including letter packets) and postcards for countries in Europe are sent by air whenever this will mean quicker delivery. It is not necessary to type the words BY AIRMAIL on the envelope.

6.3 **Letters to the Irish Republic**

R. O'Connor, Esq.,
24 Kenmore Road,
KILLARNEY,
Co. Kerry,
IRISH REPUBLIC.

TECHNIQUE DEVELOPMENT

Read the instructions for each exercise very carefully before beginning.

1 Vertical headings typed downwards

Set tab stops at 5 8 11 14 17. Type the following exercise.

```
E  A  A  A  A
U  S  F  M  U
R  I  R  E  S
O  A  I  R  T
P     C  I  R
E     A  C  A
         A  L
            A
            S
            I
            A
```

Now rule between the columns.

E	A	A	A	A
U	S	F	M	U
R	I	R	E	S
O	A	I	R	T
P		C	I	R
E		A	C	A
			A	L
				A
				S
				I
				A

Set tab stops at 5 10 15 20 25 27. Type the following exercise.

```
G    N    P    T    N I
R    E    E    A    A N
O    T    N    X    T S
S         S         I U
S    P    I         O R
     A    O         N A
P    Y    N         A N
A         S         L C
Y                     E
```

G	N	P	T	N I
R	E	E	A	A N
O	T	N	X	T S
S		S		I U
S	P	I		O R
	A	O		N A
P	Y	N		A N
A		S		L C
Y				E

2 Vertical headings typed by turning the paper horizontally.

Place a sheet of paper in your typewriter and type a horizontal line of 27 characters. Leaving *six clear linespaces*, type a second line.

English	Dutch	Swedish	Portuguese	Italian	French	German

Turn your sheet of paper horizontally, place it in your typewriter and complete the headings as shown.

4.10 **Complimentary close** Typed on second single space below the last line of the body of the letter. A letter with the salutation 'Dear Sir(s), Madam', should end 'Yours faithfully' which may be followed by the company's name. Sometimes the name of the company is typed after the signatory/designation. When a letter starts 'Dear Mr . . .', 'Dear Miss . . .', etc, the complimentary close should be 'Yours sincerely'. Never type the company's name after 'Yours sincerely', unless there are special instructions to do so. Whether you type the name and designation of the writer will depend on how well the writer knows the addressee. Follow the style in previous correspondence or ask the author.

4.11 **Name of signatory** In business letters a male person does not append the word 'Mr', before his name. However, it is common practice for ladies to put 'Miss', 'Mrs' or 'Ms' before their name or in brackets after.

4.12 **Enclosures** After the last line of typing, turn up a minimum of two spaces, and type Enc at left margin. If there is more than one enclosure, then type Encs. Some organizations list the enclosures. A few employers, and some examining bodies, prefer the abbreviation Att when the word 'attached' is used in the body of the letter, eg 'We attach a copy of our price-list.' If there is more than one attachment, a note must be made of the number, eg Att 3. Another method of indicating an enclosure, or enclosures, is to type three unspaced dots in the left margin opposite the line(s) in which the enclosure(s) is mentioned. This may not be possible with a word processor.

4.13 **Postscripts** Sometimes a postscript has to be typed at the foot of a letter, either because the writer has omitted something he wished to say in the body of the letter, or because he wishes to draw special attention to a certain point. The postscript should be started two single spaces below the last line of the complete letter and should be in single spacing. Leave two character spaces after the abbreviation. PS has no punctuation with open punctuation, but a full stop after the S with full punctuation.

4.14 **Carbon copies** It is necessary to keep in the office for filing purposes at least one carbon copy of each letter or document typed. To produce a carbon copy, take the following steps:

4.14.1 Place face downwards on a flat surface the sheet on which the typing is to be done.

4.14.2 On top of this place a sheet of carbon paper with the coated surface upwards.

4.14.3 On top of these place the sheet of paper on which the carbon copy is to be made. Pick up all sheets together and insert in machine with coated surface of carbon paper facing the cylinder.

4.14.4 All carbon copies must be a **true copy** of the original, ie any handwritten alterations made on an original must also be made on the carbon copies.

4.14.5 Many organizations do not take carbon copies; instead the originals are photocopied. When **photocopies** have to be made, it is usual to type on the original: pc or p/c followed by the number of copies required, eg pc 6.

4.15 **Additional carbon copies** In addition to the carbon copy required for filing, many business letters are typed with extra carbon copies, which are sent to any person who may be concerned. If a copy of a letter is sent to someone other than the addressee, the letters cc (carbon copy) are typed at the left margin (usually at the foot) followed by the name of the recipient. Where a copy is being sent to more than one person, the names are typed after cc one underneath the other, and the name of the person for whom the copy is intended is either ticked at the side or underlined on individual carbon copies, eg:

(First copy)	(Second copy)
cc Mr Jones	cc Mr Jones
Mrs Stone	Mrs Stone
Mr French	Mr French
File	File

(Third copy)	(Fourth copy)
cc Mr Jones	cc Mr Jones
Mrs Stone	Mrs Stone
Mr French	Mr French
File	File

4.16 **Blind carbon copies** It sometimes happens that the writer does not want the addressee to know that copies have been distributed, in which case the typist types bcc (blind carbon copy). When the letter is finished, the carbon copies are reinserted into the machine. At the foot of these copies the typist then types the bcc note at the left margin, as follows:

bcc Mr Jones
Mrs Stone
Mr French
File

marking the name of the recipient(s) as before. The bottom copy on which all the cc or bcc notes appear is the one kept for filing.

4.17 **Continuation sheets** A long letter may require a second sheet. This is called a

SKILL BUILDING 7

1 *Alphabetic sentences* Type each sentence twice.

Both sex equality and elimination of racial prejudice were taken very seriously by our organization.

In a good year the farmers harvested extra quantities of maize, in a bad one many were subject to bankruptcy.

2 *Word building* Type each row twice.

water waterproof watermark watershed watercolour waterfront waterfowl

microfiche microfilm microcomputer microwave microscope microphone

back background backhander backbench backwards backspace backlog

mail mailable airmail mailmerge mailroom mailbox mailshot mailbag

3 *Correction of spelling errors* Type each line twice correcting any errors.

agreable accommodate unnecessary courteous honorary consious

independent absense appearance budgeted colleague committee

referend efficient installment liaison maintainance negotiate

occasionally parallel embarrassed usually proceedure received

recommend secretaries seperate successfully technical tendancy

4 *Skill measurement* Target time for each exercise is 1 minute, not more than 1 error.

New recruits joining the company are put through an induction programme. This covers the products made by each division, an introduction to senior staff, and a video of the manufacturing processes. Later employees will receive information about company pensions, systems of salary payment and trade union membership.

310 keystrokes (62 words)

A clothing manufacturer has directed that all his female staff must wear the same scent. The organization employs 16 women and the MD feels strongly that the blend of all their perfumes is 'a mess'. He told the staff that they may wear his favourite perfume which costs £50 - he will supply it free of charge.

310 keystrokes (62 words)

2.2 **Open punctuation** When typing a letter with open punctuation, no punctuation marks are inserted in the reference, date, name and address of addressee, salutation, complimentary close or abbreviations. The grammatical punctuation in the body of the letter must be inserted. If a name and address appear in continuous matter, the items are separated by a comma, or two character spaces.

3 Printed heading

If you are using paper with a printed heading, turn up at least two single spaces after the last line of the printed heading before starting to type. If you are using plain A5 portrait paper, or A4 paper, turn up seven single spaces. (See also ***House Style***, page 127.)

4 Parts of a business letter

4.1 **Reference** If the words 'Our Ref' are already printed on the letterhead, type the reference in alignment with the print and leave at least **one** clear character space before typing the reference. If 'Our Ref' is not printed, turn up two single spaces after the printed letter heading and type at left margin. Turn up two single spaces and type 'Your Ref' if it is needed.

4.2 **Special marks applying to letters** The words PRIVATE, CONFIDENTIAL, PERSONAL, URGENT, RECORDED DELIVERY, REGISTERED, SPECIAL DELIVERY, BY HAND or AIRMAIL are typed at the left margin at least two single spaces after the last line of the reference, or the date, if the date is typed at the left margin. FREEPOST is typed after the name of the addressee. POSTE RESTANTE means **to be called for**. The words are typed after the name of the addressee who will collect from the post office named in the address.

4.3 **Date** Typed at least two single spaces after the reference, blocked at left margin, or typed on the same line as the reference and blocked at right margin.

4.4 **For the attention of** It is the custom with some firms to have all correspondence addressed to the firm and not to individuals. If, therefore, the writer of a letter wishes it to reach a particular person or department, the words, 'FOR THE ATTENTION OF . . .', are typed at the left margin on the second single space after the reference, date or any special instructions. The wording is also typed on the envelope two single spaces above the name and address. (**NOTE**: The salutation will, of course, be in the plural, ie Dear Sirs.)

4.5 **Name and address of addressee** (See also ***Forms of address***, page 124.) Typed in single spacing usually on the second/third single space below the reference, date, any special instructions, or 'For the attention of'.

4.5.1 May be typed in single spacing at the foot of the page at the left margin.

4.5.2 If the letter finishes with the complimentary close, turn up nine single spaces before typing the name and address of the addressee.

4.5.3 If the letter finishes with the name and designation of signatory, turn up two single spaces before typing the name and address of the addressee.

4.5.4 If you are using a continuation sheet and the name and address of addressee has not been typed before the salutation, then it may be typed at the bottom of the **first** page, two single spaces after the last typed line and ending 25 mm (1 inch) from the bottom of the page.

4.5.5 If you type the name and address of the addressee at the bottom of the page and the letter is marked for the attention of a particular person, the attention line is typed before the salutation. Similarly, any special instructions must be typed in the usual place and not at the bottom of the page.

4.5.6 In a one-page letter with the name and address of the addressee at the bottom, the enclosure notation should be placed two spaces after the last line of the address.

4.6 **Salutation** Typed on the second single space below the last line of the address and blocked at the left margin. If the correspondent wishes to write the salutation in ink, leave plenty of space. It is suggested that you turn up nine single spaces after the last line of the address before starting the body of the letter.

4.7 **Subject heading** In fully-blocked letters, the subject heading is typed at the left margin, preferably in capitals without underscore. If lower case letters are used, the heading should be underscored. The heading must be centred if the indented style of display is being used.

4.8 **Body of letter** Start on the second single space after the salutation or the subject heading.

4.9 **Displayed matter** When matter is to be displayed in a fully-blocked letter, all the lines usually start at the left margin, one clear space left above and below the matter. If the display is in columns, it is usual to leave three spaces between each column. If definite instructions are given for the matter to be inset, then it must be inset, even in a fully-blocked letter. The matter is usually centred in a semi-blocked letter.

Exercise 1

Type the following table on plain A4 paper. Type the vertical headings as shown.

COMPARATIVE INSURANCE COSTS[1]

Standard Service	Description of Standard Service	SPAIN	FRANCE	ITALY	LUXEMBOURG	NETHERLANDS	UK
Life Assurance	Average Annual Cost of ^Term^ (Life) Assurance	67	63	113	96	23	0
Home Insurance	Annual Cost of Theft/Fire Cover	-94	-51	-9	-33	-63	0
Motor Ins	Annual Cost of Comprehensive Policy – NCB[2] – 10 yrs, 1.6l car	117	26	165	94	10	0
Commercial Fire & Theft	Annual Cover for Premises & Stock Valued at 600,485 ECU[3]	-3	126	~~128~~ 218	~~-41~~ -42	-28	0

2 NCB = No Claims Bonus

3 ECU = European Currency Units

1 Percentage variations w the UK as a standard of 0

the border too heavy, as this will detract from the general appearance.

```
* * * * * *    0: 0: 0: 0: 0: 0    ***      ***
*         *    :              :    *          *
* * * * * *    :              :    *          *
               0: 0: 0: 0: 0: 0    *          *
                                   *          *
                                   ***      ***
```

Brief notes

You may be asked, in the office or in an examination, to type a letter or memo from brief notes. The following procedure should be adopted:

1 Type a rough draft, making sure you get the points in the correct order, usually in the order they are given in the brief notes.
2 Avoid short, disconnected sentences and decide where to paragraph.
3 There is no need to correct typing errors in the rough draft as it will waste time, but verify dates, people's names, etc, and type them accurately.
4 Remove paper from machine and read very carefully what you have typed, making any further amendments that may be necessary.
5 Insert a fresh sheet of paper, with appropriate carbon copies, and type a final copy ready for despatch.

Bring forward reminders

Very often it is important for a person to ascertain by a particular date that a certain action has been taken. The action may be the result of outgoing correspondence, incoming correspondence, a telephone call, etc. A special file, which has a variety of names such as bring-forward file, bring-up file, tickler file, follow-up file, etc, is kept for this purpose.

As a typist it may be one of your duties to keep a bring-forward file, and for that purpose you may have a concertina file with a space for each month of the year and, at the front, pockets for each day of the current month. In the various sections you will keep papers, documents and notes, that require attention on a particular date. At the end of each month, you should transfer the contents of the next month's pocket into the daily pockets. You must train yourself to look in the bring-up file each morning and take out that day's reminders so that action may be taken. Your employer may ask you to make a note, on a file copy or on a special copy kept for the purpose, of the date on which a certain document should be brought forward.

Business letters

1 Layout

Letters can be displayed in various ways, the styles most commonly used are illustrated below.

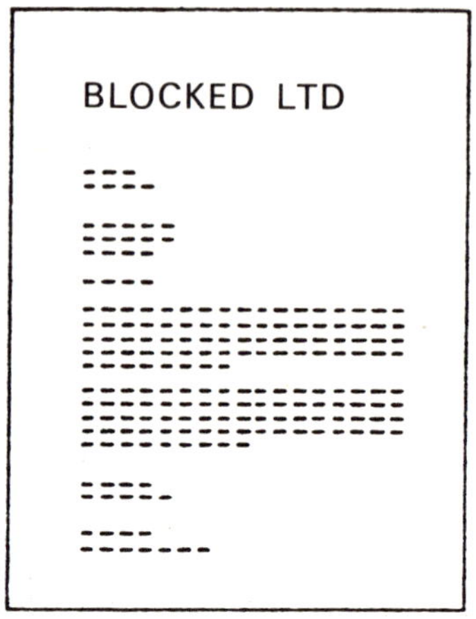

Fully-blocked (sometimes called 'blocked').

Begin every line at the left margin.

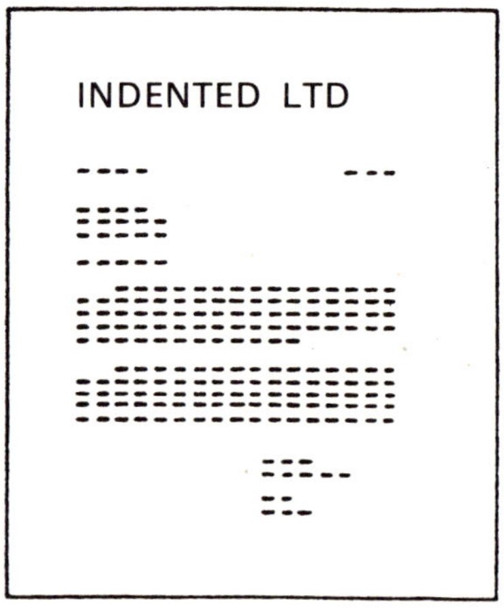

Semi-blocked (sometimes called 'indented').

Date and complimentary close as shown, with first line of each paragraph indented.

2 Punctuation

2.1 **Full punctuation** When typing a letter with full punctuation, punctuation marks are inserted in the appropriate places in the reference, date, name and address of addressee, salutation, complimentary close and after all abbreviations.

Exercise 2

Type the following table on A5 portrait paper.

REGENT CREST HOTEL, LEAMINGTON SPA

ROOM CAPACITIES

(Please type in lower case with initial capital →) SEATING ARRANGEMENT

SEATING ARRANGEMENT	Crest Suite	Regent Suite	Shakespeare Room	Arden Room	~~Coltbor~~ Cobden Rm
Classroom	–	24	40	–	50
Boardroom	16	18	30	–	–
U-Shaped	12	18	–	–	–
Theatre	36	55	70	95	120

(Shakespeare Room ↔ Cobden Rm)

Type the vertical headings downwards, as in exercise 1.

Exercise 3

Type the following skeleton table on plain A4 paper. Rule as shown.

SWITCHBOARD ~~AREA~~ ROT

MONDAY		TUES →		and so on up to Friday →
am	pm	am	pm	→
Leave 12 lines spaces				

adjusted by means of the paper release lever to the correct position for the addition or alteration. The necessary correction is then made.

5 If the letters next to the alteration are light (when rubbing out you may have also rubbed over the adjacent letters) type over these so that all letters are the same shade.

Backing sheet

To prevent damage to the cylinder of the typewriter, always use a backing sheet. Other uses of the backing sheet are:

1 Typing on cards and memoranda

When typing on cards and memoranda, you may have, of necessity, to type near the bottom. To ensure that your typewriter grips the card (paper) and thus prevents the bottom line(s) from 'running off' the paper, always use a backing sheet. In fact, whenever you have to type within 25 mm (1 inch) of the bottom, always use a backing sheet which extends below the bottom of the page.

2 Aid to centring

On your backing sheet rule a vertical line down the centre and also a heavy horizontal line across the centre. This will help you when centring material on a page.

3 Top and bottom margins

With the underscore type a line on the seventh single space from the top edge of the paper. This will remind you that you always turn up seven single spaces before you start to type. Likewise, 25 mm (1 inch) from the bottom of the backing sheet draw a dark horizontal line to remind you that you are nearing the bottom of the page.

Balance sheets

See ***Financial statements***, page 120.

Bibliography

A bibliography is a list of books, magazines, or newspaper articles, included in footnotes at the end of a chapter or book to show the source from which the information has been taken or as a reading list for people who want to go further into the subject. The items are listed alphabetically according to the author's last name which is typed in upper and lower case. The author's name is typed first followed by the forename(s) or initials. With full punctuation, use the comma and full stops as follows:

Drummond, A. M. and Coles-Mogford, A., *Typing First Course*, McGraw-Hill, Maidenhead, 1988.

With blocked style, it is usual to block all lines although the second and subsequent lines for any one item may be inset five to ten spaces. The titles of the books are typed in upper and lower case and underlined, or in sloping type, because the printer will set them in italic.

Bills of quantities

A bill of quantities is a document showing the details and prices of materials to be used in building, etc. Its purpose is to obtain tenders for the work to be done and materials required. It also enables the architect to make an accurate estimate of the work to be carried out.

A4 paper is used and the vertical lines are ruled over the full length of the paper. Follow the layout given. When typing between the vertical lines, every endeavour should be made to see that the characters do not touch the lines.

Short bills of quantities are folded from left to right and endorsed on the uppermost side, ie with folded edge to the left. Long bills of quantities are bound and endorsed on the front page.

Bold print

Most electronic machines have a facility that enables the operator to print characters with a much darker type than the normal printing. This emboldening is a very useful device for emphasizing text.

Borders (*ornamental*)

Display work, such as programmes, menus, etc, can be made more artistic by the use of a suitable ornamental border or corners, such as shown on page 108. You should be able to make up other artistic borders, but in doing so, take care not to make

Exercise 4

Type the following table on A5 portrait paper.

MADE TO MEASURE SERVICES

Fabric Type[1]	Curtains[2]	Pelmets	Festoon Blinds	Cushion Covers	Upholstery
Cotton	x	x	x	x	
Chintz	x	x	x	x	x
Velveteen	x			x	x

1 For prices see list 8/92. We supply up to 3 fabric swatches without charge.

2 Ask the assistant for advice regarding measurements, or phone our free advisory service on 01-444-9811

Please set out as

	Fabric Type: Cotton, Chintz, etc
Curtains . . . etc	

use leader dots

Type the vertical headings downwards, as in exercise 1.

Exercise 5

Type the following table on A5 landscape paper.

LABOUR ANALYSIS

please change dashes to 0s except in the final column, as indicated.

Production Department — Mth End: Aug

Employee Group	Total as at 31/7	Starters: Recruits	Starters: Transfers	Starters: Total	Leavers: Terminations	Leavers: Transfers	Leavers: Total	Increase or Decrease: +	Increase or Decrease: − (RETAIN)
Skilled	572	~~7~~ 6	—	~~7~~ 6	14	—	14		~~7~~ 8
Semi-skilled	371	14	2	16	12	1	13	3	
Unskilled	926	6	—	6	14	4	18		12
YTS	24	24	—	24	3	1	4	20	
P/t	17	1	1	2	—	—	0	2	

(YTS and P/t rows to be transposed)

Type the vertical headings downwards, as in exercise 1.

The word AGENDA is blocked at the left margin or centred on the writing line, usually in spaced capitals. The numbers may be blocked or, if indented from the left margin, the longest line may end the same number of spaces from the right margin.

Align

To arrange typed letters in a straight line. If the base of a character appears above or below the normal line of type, it is said to be out of alignment. This is most unsightly and should be avoided at all costs. Also, to align vertically means that all lines start at the same scale point.

Aligned right margin

Programmes, display, financial statements, etc, sometimes have a right column and the last character of each line of this column may have to end at the same scale point. To do this:

Decide on the exact scale point at which you wish the last character to be typed, and set a tab stop one space to the right of that point. From the tab stop, backspace once for each character and space in the line to be aligned; from the point reached, type the word(s)/figure(s). This is sometimes referred to as justifying, but justifying really means inserting extra spaces between words so that the lines of the text all end at the same scale point. Electronic machines may have a 'flush right' facility to allow the information to be typed so that it will end automatically at the right margin.

Alignment scale (sometimes known as line indicators)

Close to the cylinder, behind the ribbon on each side of the printing point, there are a number of vertical marks, the tops of which indicate the base of the typing line. This scale is sometimes located on the clear-view card holder. Also, a red vertical line in the top centre of the card holder indicates where the next character will print vertically on the paper. There are a variety of indicators on electronic typewriters.

Allocating space

You may be asked to leave blank spaces for the insertion of photographs, etc, or you may have to draw geometrical figures. The diagram or blank space left must be the exact size indicated. For instance, if you were asked to leave a **blank** space of 51 mm (2 inches) you should turn up 13 (**thirteen**) single linespaces. However, if you have to **insert lines** and use the **underscore** for the horizontals, you would turn up the exact number of lines. For example, if you had to draw a square 51 mm (2 inches) deep, and you were using the underscore for the horizontal lines, you would type the first horizontal line, turn up 12 (**twelve**) and type the second horizontal line.

Horizontal and vertical lines may be drawn in ink or by means of the underscore. Alternatively, the horizontal lines may be typed by the underscore and the vertical lines drawn in ink, provided the ink is the same colour as the lines typed by the underscore.

When typing from complicated copy, it is a good plan to type a draft quickly to see how much space the typing, drawing, etc, is likely to take up. When a diagram has typing before and after it, there should be a blank space before the first line and after the last line.

Amendments to text

Draft work, whether typewritten or handwritten, invariably contains amendments in some form. This can include matter to be transferred from one portion of the text to another, items deleted and replaced with other information, an instruction to insert a new paragraph, to type words or lines in capital letters or spaced capitals, etc. Most work in offices, and in examinations, will be edited in some way, and it is part of the typist's job to be able to interpret these amendments and make the necessary corrections. Time spent in reading and understanding the copy will mean speedier and more accurate presentation of the final document.

Back-feeding

It sometimes happens that an addition or alteration has to be made to a page of a document consisting of several sheets which have been stapled together. This can be done (without having to unfasten the sheets) by what is known as 'backward feed', ie inserting the paper into the machine from the front of the cylinder instead of in the normal manner.

To do this, the following steps should be taken.

1 Erase neatly any letter(s) that have to be altered.
2 Insert a single sheet of paper in the machine in the usual way.
3 Between the sheet of paper just inserted and the cylinder, insert the bottom of the page to be altered.
4 Turn the cylinder backwards so that the two sheets are fed together sufficiently far for the loose sheet to be removed. The typewritten sheet, on which the alteration is to be made, is held firmly by the feed mechanism and it can be

Exercise 6

Type the following table on A4 portrait paper.

FOOD FACTS & FALACIES

The table below lists the nutritional value of 100 g.*

	Protein	Carbohydrate	Fibre	Fat	Calories	Vitamins & Minerals
*Almonds	16.9	4.3	14.3	53.5	565	B1 B2 B3 Fo E Ca Fe K Mg P Zn
*Brazil Nuts	12.0	4.1	9.0	61.5	619	B1 B3 B6 E Ca Fe K Mg P Zn
Broad Beans	4.1	7.1	4.2	0.6	48	B3
Butter Beans	7.1	17.1	5.1	0.3	95	K Zn
Haricot Beans	6.6	16.6	7.4	0.5	93	Fe Mg Zn
*Hazelnuts	7.6	6.8	6.1	36.0	380	B1 B6 Fo E Mg P Zn
Lentils	7.6	17.0	2.7	0.5	99	B6 Fe
*Peanuts	24.3	8.6	8.1	49.0	570	B1 B3 B6 Fo E K Mg P Zn
Red Kidney Beans	7.8	21.4	8.6	0.5	118	F
Soya Flour	36.8	23.5	11.9	23.5	447	B1 B2 B3 B6 Ca Fe K Mg P
*Walnuts	10.6	5.0	5.2	51.5	525	B1 B3 B6 Fo Fe K Mg Zn

Key (Minerals)

Ca = Calcium Fe = Iron K = Potassium Mg = Magnesium P = Phosphorus
Zn = Zinc Fo = Folic Acid ← list in alphabetical order and type down the page

* Please note that details of vitamins and minerals are only given where significant quantities occur.

* Typist - please prepare this table with items indicated * only.

Type B vitamins (B1, B2, B3, B6) with the number as a subscript - B_1 B_2 B_3 etc.

4.3 **Used with figures only**

am (a.m.)	= *ante meridiem* = before noon
HP (H.P.)	= hire purchase
No, Nos (No., Nos.)	= number, numbers
pm (p.m.)	= *post meridiem* = after noon
% (%)	= per centum
v, vol (v., vol.)	= volume
*in (in.)	= inch or inches
ft (ft.)	= foot or feet
*oz (oz.)	= ounce or ounces
*lb (lb.)	= pound or pounds (weight)
*cwt (cwt.)	= hundredweight or hundredweights
*m	= metre, metres
*mm	= millimetre, millimetres
*cm	= centimetre, centimetres
*g	= gram, grams
*kg	= kilogram, kilograms

* These do not require an s in the plural.

NOTE: It would seem preferable to add an s for the plural of yd and qr (yds/yds. qrs/qrs.). This style is recommended by the *Oxford Dictionary for Writers and Editors*; however, the British Standards Institution gives both examples without the s. Follow the author's copy and/or house style.

4.4 **Used in cases indicated**

& (&)	= ampersand = and. Used in names of firms and numbers [Nos 25 & 26 (Nos. 25 & 26)] never in ordinary matter.
BA (B.A.)	= Bachelor of Arts. Degree after a person's name.
Bros (Bros.)	= Brothers. In names of firms or companies only.
bf (b.f.)	= brought forward (accounting) or boldface (word processing)
c/o (c/o)	= care of. Used only in addresses. (Sometimes the word 'at' is used instead of c/o.)
Co (Co.)	= Company. Used in names of companies.
cod (c.o.d.) COD (C.O.D.)	= Cash on delivery. Used on invoices.
DSc (D.Sc.)	= Doctor of Science. Degree after person's name.
E & OE (E. & O.E.)	= Errors and omissions excepted. Used in invoices.
Jnr (Jnr.)	= Junior. Used in addresses after a man's name to distinguish from senior [Snr (Snr.)].
Ltd (Ltd.)	= Limited. Used in the name of a private limited company.
PS (PS.)	= Postscript. Abbreviated form used at end of letter and memo only.
PLC (P.L.C.) plc (p.l.c.)	= Public Limited Company. Used after the name of public limited company.
pro tem (pro tem.)	= *pro tempore* (for the time being). Used after a designation, eg Secretary pro tem.
Ref (Ref.)	= Reference. Used in letters and memos.
SERPS	= State Earnings Related Pension Scheme. (May be in full or abbreviated.)

Accents

When a typewriter is used for a great deal of foreign correspondence, the keys are usually fitted with the necessary accents. However, when accents are used only occasionally, the following are put in by hand in the same coloured ink as the ribbon:

acute grave circumflex tilde

Usually typed as combination characters are:

diaeresis and umlaut = quotation marks (") typed over letter;

cedilla = type letter c, backspace and type comma.

For examples see page 144.

Agenda

When the notice of a meeting is sent out, it is normal practice to include the agenda, which is a list of items to be discussed at a meeting, these being listed in a certain order and numbered for easy reference as follows:

1 Apologies
2 Minutes of the last meeting
3 Matters arising out of the minutes
4 Correspondence
5 Reports
6 Any special points for discussion
7 Any other business
8 Date of next meeting

As is the notice of a meeting, the agenda is sent to all who are entitled to attend. It is usually duplicated and care should be taken to run off additional copies for members who may forget to bring a copy to a meeting.

Exercise 7

Type the following table on A4 paper.

Please type management in full throughout

NORTHERN GROUP MGT TRAINING

VIDEOS & FILMS [for hire] AS AT (insert today's date)

Create a sep column for the ref nos - don't include the brackets

TITLE	Ref No	Film Version	~~Film~~ Video Version	Playback Facilities
General Mgt				
Coping w Stress (GM44)				
Harmonization of Working Conditions (GM3)				
Managing Meetings (GM20)				
In Search of Excellence (GM14)				
Managing Change (GM11)				
Time Mgt (GM12)				
Interviewing Skills (GM1)				
Customer Care				
Making Cold Calls (CC4)				
PR - Everyone's Bus (CC20)				
In the Customer's Shoes (CC3)				
Awkward Customers? (CC14)				
Financial Mgt				
Budgeting (FM1)				
Cost, Profit & Breakeven (FM4)				
Depreciation & Inflation (FM2)				
Controlling Cash Flow (FM6)				
Ratio Analysis (FM9)				

* Please tick yr requirements

Please type the titles in ascending numerical order of ref no within each section.

DATA BANK

This **Data bank** is in alphabetical order and gives up-to-date, precise and clear information about typewriting conventions, display and layout—in other words, **a guide** to present-day practices and document presentation.

Abbreviations

In typewritten work, abbreviations should not, as a rule, be used. There are, however, a few which are **never** typed in full, and others which may be used in certain circumstances.

1 Open and full punctuation

When using **open** punctuation, no full stops are inserted after initials or in abbreviations, eg Mrs Y W T St George-Stevens is Managing Director of Y W T Stevens & Co Ltd. With **full** punctuation, full stops are inserted after initials and in abbreviations, eg Mrs. Y. W. T. St. George-Stevens is Managing Director of Y. W. T. Stevens & Co. Ltd.

Notice the spacing in the following:

Open punctuation Mrs S J Hudson MA BSc—where an abbreviation consists of two or more letters, there is no space between the letters but one space between each group of letters. **Full** punctuation Mrs. S. J. Hudson, M.A., B.Sc.—space between the groups is replaced by a comma, followed by a clear space.

1.1 However, with **full** punctuation, full stops need not be inserted in the following cases:
  - 1.1.1 **Acronyms** (words formed from initials): VAT, PAYE, UNESCO, NATO, BUPA, OPEC, NUPE, ACAS, etc.
  - 1.1.2 **Names** of **well-known** companies, states, countries, radio and television broadcasting stations, unions and many government departments: ICI, GKN, USA, UK, RSA, EEC, BBC, IBS, DES, etc.
  - 1.1.3 In metric measurements: 12 mm, 4 m, 6 kg, 30 km, etc.

2 Imperial measurements

No punctuation is inserted with open punctuation, but with full punctuation the full stops are inserted, eg 2 lb., 2 ft. 4 in.

3 Longhand abbreviations

These are used in handwriting, but the words must be typed in full. Examples: dept = department; st = street; shd = should; sh = shall; w = will; wh = which; th = that; etc. Great care must be taken to verify the correct spelling when typing abbreviations in full, eg accom = accommodation; gntee(s) = guarantee(s); recd = received; def = definitely; sep = separate; rec(s) = receipt(s); temp = temporary; etc. Days of the week and months of the year, eg Wed, Fri, Jan, Sept, etc, **must** be typed in full. Where the names of persons, towns, countries, associations, etc, are repeated in any group of tasks, the author may write only the initial(s) or use the initial(s) followed by a long dash to represent the word(s). For example: in a letter addressed to Mrs R Green, the handwritten salutation may read, Dear Mrs G———, and the typist would be expected to type Dear Mrs Green.

4 Standard abbreviations

Lists of standard abbreviations, with their uses, are given below. Study the lists so that you will know when and when not to use the abbreviations. Full punctuation is given in brackets, although the tendency today is to use open punctuation.

4.1 **Common abbreviations** Usually abbreviated, but may be typed in full. It is wise to follow the style used by the author and/or house style. **Be consistent.**

Ecu	= European currency unit
EMS	= European Monetary System
Hon Sec (Hon. Sec.)	= Honorary Secretary. Typed in full.
IQPS (I.Q.P.S.)	= Institute of Qualified Private Secretaries
MEP (M.E.P.)	= Member of the European Parliament
MoD (M.o.D.)	= Ministry of Defence
mph (m.p.h.)	= miles per hour
RMO (R.M.O.)	= Resident Medical Officer
RNLI (R.N.L.I.)	= Royal National Lifeboat Institution
SCF (S.C.F.)	= Save the Children Fund
WCT (W.C.T.)	= World Championship Tennis
(U.K.R.O.F.S.)	= United Kingdom Register of Organic Food Standards

4.2 **Always used**

ad lib (ad lib.)	= *ad libitum*	= at pleasure
eg (e.g.)	= exempli gratia	= for example
Esq (Esq.)	= Esquire	= courtesy title
etc (etc.)	= et cetera	= and others
et seq (et seq.)	= *et sequentes*	= and the following
ie (i.e.)	= *id est*	= that is
Messrs (Messrs.)	= Messieurs	= courtesy title
Mr (Mr.)	= Mister	= courtesy title
Mrs (Mrs.)		= courtesy title
NB (N.B.)	= *Nota bene*	= note well

SKILL BUILDING 8

1 *Alphabetic sentences* Type each sentence twice.

The extraordinary mix of guests invited back to the July festivities was quite a puzzle to them all.

The snack bar was frequently judged to sell excellent pizzas with a variety of toppings of meat, fish and vegetables.

2 *Word building* Type each row twice.

stock stockist stockbroker stockholder stockroom stocktaking stockout

account accountancy accountant accountable accounting accountability

ever however every everything everywhere everybody everyday everyone

out outside outskirts outstanding output outlook outline outlet buyout

3 *Correction of errors* Each sentence contains *at least* five word errors. Read each sentence, check spellings and then type each sentence correctly.

1 We were suprised to recieve seperate notification of a further delivery from there Leceister Works.

2 The principle reason for loosing such an excellent secretery seems to have been the negative attutude of the personal officer.

3 The days itinery includes a talk by our recently-apointed Managment ADvisor and lunch in the restuarant.

4 *Production development from manuscript*

Reading time: 1 minute Target typing time: 2 minutes

1 of Europes oldest cities, Cologne, claims to be Germany's most remarkable post-war miracle – a phoenix ~~that has~~ risen from the ashes! [In 1945 70% of the city lay in ruins; in the ~~historic~~ central area, the devastation was almost total. Yet, within a few decades, the ancient centre ~~of the city~~ has been rebuilt, retaining ~~much of~~ its quaint medaeval atmosphere. [Today its a thriving industrial + commercial centre. It is also becoming increasingly popular w tourists – the narrow streets of the old town are bustling w activity, and are located close to a major area of ~~tourists~~ tourist accom near the Rhine.

600 keystrokes (120 words)

FASH

Gross Profit	37,037	26,723
Distribution Costs	5,524	3,437

FUNDS

Payment of tax	80,000
Payment of dividends	50,000
Trade creditors	52,500

GUIDE

F8 SAVE work on disc but continue with
current document
ALT + F8 Save work on disc and return to
main menu
F9 FIND and REPLACE (manual and global)

MENU

Wines: St-Georges-St-Emilion (1988)
Gewurztraminer (1989)

STAND

SP1 You should assume that your application has not been successful if you have not heard from us within 2 weeks.

SP2 Please attach your advertisement securely to this form and send in the internal mail to Richard Drew, Publication Department.

SP3 For further information contact Denise Woolley at P & R Publicity on (0203) 44992.

SP4 Thank you for your letter dated with which you enclosed a cheque for

VITAE

Date of Birth: 15 May 56
Marital Status: Single
Nationality: British

GRANT ARCHER & ASSOCIATES

OFFICE SERVICES – REQUEST FORM

This sheet contains instructions that must be complied with when typing the documents. Read the information carefully before starting, and refer back to it frequently.

Typist's log sheet

Originator Richard Morrison   Department Information Technology Services   Date   Ext No 440

Typists operating a word processor, or electronic typewriter with appropriate function keys, should apply the following automatic facilities: top margin; carrier return; line-end hyphenation; underline OR bold print (embolden); error correction; centring; any other relevant applications.

Remember to (a) complete the details required at the bottom of the form; (b) enter typing time per document in the appropriate column; and (c) before submitting this **log sheet** and your completed work, enter TOTAL TYPING TIME in the last column so that the typist's time may be charged to the originator.

Document No	Type of document and instructions	Copies – Original plus	Input form¶	Typing time per document	Total typing time ¥
1	Customer Enquiry Details form	top copy only	M/S		
2	Memo to Alan Walker	Top + 2	M/S		
3	Itinerary for Channel Islands visit	top copy only	M/S		
4	Useful Contacts table – more names to follow	top copy only	M/S		
* 5 urgent	Letter to Applied Technology Inc + envelope (please sign and despatch immediately)	top + 1	M/S		
6	Printer's table	top copy only	AT		
			TOTAL	TYPING TIME	

TYPIST – please complete:

Typist's name: Date received: Date completed:

Time received: Time completed:

If the typed documents cannot be returned within 24 hours, the office services supervisor should inform the originator. Any item that is urgent should be marked with an asterisk (*).

¶ T = Typescript   AT = Amended Typescript   MS = Manuscript   SD = Shorthand Dictation   AD = Audio Dictation

¥ To be charged to the originator's department.

DATA FILES

The following office files contain information that you will need when typing certain documents.

AGEN

7 AOB
8 Date of next meeting

ALPHA

APPLETON Sara
APPLIED Technology Inc PO Box 414 Charing Cross St Helier Jersey CI
ARDEN House Hotel Station Road Kenilworth Warwickshire CV44 8TX
BERGEN Dr J 56 Field View Lane Cuffley Herts EN6 4JQ
BRAY Roger
BYRNE Hazel Chief Executive SRN Network plc PO Box 414 Marlow Bucks SL7 1YW
COOKE Neil Neil Cooke (Roofing) Ltd 399 Showell Green Lane Sparkhill Birmingham B11 5UB
DAWOOD Nigel General Manager RPM Radio plc 245 Baker Street London W1N 9YB
DEVLIN Michael Accounts Grant Archer Management Consultants
DIAMOND Jenny BQB Promotions 223 Broadleach Lane Ipswich Suffolk IP4 8HN
ELLIS Brian Chief Accountant
GRANT Archer & Associates Cromwell House Great Rissington Cheltenham Glos GL54 3TN
HOWELL Robert 30 Greenslade Road Harborne Birmingham B17 5QW
HUNT Barry Managing Director
JACKSON George Production Manager
JONES Karen Property Division
LEWIS Richard Marketing Manager Grant Archer Management Consultants
LONDON Transport plc 55 The Broadway London SW1H 0HD
MEDIA Premiere 200 London Road Reading Berks RG1 4PT Telephone (0734) 59511/4
MORTON Graeme 45 The Quadrant Brighton BN2 1PT
PHELPS M 2 Stanley Croft Medomsley Consett Co Durham DH8 6QP
PINTER Mike
P & R Publicity Telephone (0203) 44992
ROSE Richard
SS Publications Freemans Way Leicester LE1 3SP Telephone (0503) 445501
VERNON Graham TWX Designs 11 Castle Mews Kenilworth Warwickshire CV44 9YP Telephone (0926) 339920
VIDEO Presentations Ltd FREEPOST London NE1L 4GT
WALKER Terry
WILLIS Neil Telephone (0926) 339920

APPEN

Departmental Revenue	2.65
Reduced Publicity	16.30
Abolition	100

DUBAI

(c) the limited opportunities for contact with other Europeans;
(d) that we are in a position to offer single status accommodation only.

15 mins

1 Customer Enquiry Details Grant Archer & Associates

Name .... Position ....

Co. ....

Address ....

Tel No. .... Extention ....

Grant Archer Services (please tick) as many as you wish

☐	Information Technology	☐	Export Management Services
☐	Training	☐	Management Search/Selection
☐	Co Relocation	☐	Public Relations

☐ Plse let me have more info ~~..~~ about ~~..~~ what G— A— has to offer in the areas indicated above.

☐ Plse ask a representative to contact me direct.

2 Memo to Alan Walker — Rymers plc (15 mins) (use shoulder headings)

1. Poss EPOS Contract I had lunch w Rex Urquhart of the Nottingham retailing group, Rymers plc, yesterday. He tells me that his Board is about to ~~authorise~~ ~~recom~~ a pilot EPOS study along the lines of our Channel Islands venture.

2. Supplier Database. Can you let me have a list of software houses wh have demonstrated this sort of expertise on an international front.

It seems likely that we sh be ~~awarded~~ given the contract (initially worth about £50,000. [Currently Rymers have 28 UK department stores w subsidiary operations in Belgium & Canada. Expansion throughout the EEC looks likely in the near future; plse do a search on this while I am away in the Channel Isles.

cc Jane Stewart (for info only)

Page 76

Recall the document stored under filename VITAE. Block the longest line and start all lines at the same scale point. Centre vertically for printout on A5 portrait paper. Proofread and, if necessary, correct. Print out one original and one carbon copy on A5 portrait paper in *12 pitch*. On the other pages of the document stored under filename VITAE change the margins so that the document will fit on to two pages of A5 portrait paper. Add the courtesy title Mr before Nigel Dawood's name and the courtesy title Ms before Hazel Byrne's name. Proofread and, if necessary, correct. Print out one original and one carbon copy on A5 portrait paper in *12 pitch*.

Page 79

Recall the document stored under filename MARR. Make the lettered shoulder headings into lettered paragraph headings. Enter the particulars for the marriage of JAMES NEIL GARDINER to SHARON JANE MARTIN on 4 June 1991. The fee for the ceremony is £48. The right margin should not be justified. Proofread and, if necessary, correct. Print out one original and one carbon copy in 12 pitch.

(30 mins)

3 Itinery ~~Visi~~ Visit to Channel Islands, (Guernsey & Jersey)
14-16th Oct. Richard Morrison & Nigel Travers

← Mon 14 Oct

10 O'clock Depart Bugford (by car)
12 noon Arrive Heathrow Airport
131~~4~~7 Dep Heathrow Airport - British Airways (Terminal 1, flight no BA 441)
1353 Arr States Airport (Guernsey). Take taxi to Victoria Hotel, ↙Peter Port (St)
1530 Meeting W Jacques Depin & Pierre Vinois of Complete Systems (CI) Ltd - foyer of Victoria Hotel
1930 Dinner at ~~Le Fregate~~ Château D'Audrien Restuarant W Jacques D—, Pierre V— & ~~Brian~~ Jo Slater (M.D of Complete Systems (CI) Ltd) ^[JO]

Tue 15 Oct
0945 Dep Victoria Hotel (by taxi) ← (10 o'clock arrive States Airport (Guernsey))
1030 Dep S-A-(G)- Aurigney Airlines [AURIGNEY]
1100 Arr S-A-(Jersey) Take taxi to the Pomme D'Or Hotel, St Helier
1230 Lunch W Michael Jones & Harry Watson of Applied Technology Inc. ~~Waterside Ristaurant~~ (The Count House) St Helier
1430 Tour of instalation (to be arranged ~~by Applied Tech Inc~~)
1630 Return to hotel
1800 Meeting followed by dinner at the Pomme D'Or Hotel W Carol Waites & Richard Lewis (De-Luce) to discuss proposed EPoS installation.

Wed 16/10
0845 ~~Taxi to airport~~ Dep Pomme d'or Hotel, Jersey (taxi to airport)
1000 Dep S—A—(J) Fl No BA983
1042 Arr London (Heathrow Airport)

TEXT EDITING INSTRUCTIONS

Page 11
Recall the document stored under filename MENU. Centre the longest line and start all lines at the same scale point. Remove the underline from the main heading. Proofread soft copy and, if necessary, correct. Print out one original in 12 pitch.

Page 17
Recall the document stored under filename VIDEO. Change to blocked paragraphs and put the towns in alphabetical order. The leader lines after **Name** should extend to the right margin and the word **Company** should have a line to itself. Proofread soft copy and, if necessary, correct. Print out one original in 10 pitch.

Page 35
Recall the document stored under filename SHORT. Replace the arabic numbers with lower case letters in brackets: (a) (b) etc. and leave two clear spaces after the brackets. In the text, all numbers should be in words. Proofread soft copy and, if necessary, correct. Print out one original in 10 pitch.

Page 39
Recall the document stored under filename PRESS. Centre main heading and change the double spacing to single spacing. The paragraph starting **Grant Systems PLC** should come before the paragraph starting **Marketing Director Keith Grant says**. Proofread soft copy and, if necessary, correct. Print out one original in 12 pitch.

Page 41
Recall the document stored under filename CHAIR. Delete numbers 1 to 4 and start the shoulder headings at the left margin. Delete the ruled box and leave the space blank. Make a global search to find every occurrence of the word **year** and embolden the word immediately preceding it. Proofread soft copy and, if necessary, correct. Print out one original and two carbon copies in 15 pitch.

Page 59
Recall the document stored under filename BOXES. Increase the character spaces to the left and right of the boxes. The words **Job Design** should be in all capitals and centred in the box. Proofread soft copy and, if necessary, correct. Print out one original in 10 pitch.

Page 67
Recall the document stored under filename FINAN. The information under **CLCS Pilot Project** should be lettered (b), and (b) should be lettered (a). This means that **TACK Project** comes before **CLCS Pilot Project**. The rate of pay per day should read £350. In both cases, alter the extensions and the totals. Proofread and, if necessary, correct. Print out one original and one carbon copy in *10 pitch*.

Page 68
Recall the document stored under filename SHARE. Transpose the columns headed **Total** and **Group Percentage**. Put in two additional spaces between the two columns. Proofread and, if necessary, correct. Print out one original in 10 pitch.

Page 72
Recall the document stored under filename GUIDE. Leave an extra two spaces after the boxes and before the start of the paragraphs. After the paragraph ending . . . **page numbering** leave 38 mm ($1\frac{1}{2}$ inches) clear before starting **F4**. Delete the underline from all words typed in closed capitals. Proofread and, if necessary, correct. Print out one original in 12 pitch.

Page 74
Recall the document stored under filename CHECK. Start the second page with **3 PUBLICITY** and make it number 4 and renumber. Number 3 will be added later at the bottom of page 1. Delete the last column headed **COMPLETED BY (DATE)**. Proofread and, if necessary, correct. Print out one original in 12 pitch.

(30 mins)

(4) Colin Jackson, Mortgage & Investment Broker, Castle Chambers, 150 St Faith's Lane, Norwich, NR2 9TQ (Colin Jackson)

Alan J Brunton, Morris Bros PLC, Green Bank Works, Leeds, LS2 9HG

Anne Rogers, KXRA Computer Systems, The Baltic Centre, Gt West Rd, Brentford, Mddx. TW8 9BU

Micro Software Ltd, Chase Close, Chantry Industrial Estate, Bedford, MK42 7SG (Keith Watkins)

Heinz Berzau [BERZAU], Country Developers, Wandle Way, Mitcham, Surrey, CR4 4NB 01-640-59117

J.P. Saddleworth & Co Consultants, Talbot House, The Square, (Simon Jolliffe) Stow-on-the-Wold, Cheltenham, Glos. GL54 1AB (0451) 76294

Barry Challenor, Mayhew Ltd, 344 Guild St, Stratford-upon-Avon, Warwickshire CV37 6QY (0789) 297104

Stella Watkin, F.W. Booth plc, Strand House, London SW1P 4RA

Jack Pemberton, Key Systems Ltd, New Street, B'ham, B9 4DS (021 742 2677)

Woods & Co (Martin Gostin [GOSTIN]) 12 Witney Rd, Oxford OX2 7ED

Plse prepare a table of these contacts in alphabetical order of company

USEFUL CONTACTS

Company	Contact Name	Post Town	Postcode
Booth F W plc etc ↓			

TIMED SKILL MEASUREMENT 5

keystrokes

On 5 January, having dealt with the morning's paperwork in order to leave 75
outstanding business matters in manageable form, Mr Connell left the office 152
at 1030 hours with the object of driving to London, a journey which 220
normally took just over 3 hours. However, with fog on the motorway, and 2 295
lengthy delays due to contraflows, it was 1500 hours before he reached the 369
outskirts of London, and a further hour before he located the Embassy 440
building in Queens Gate, SW7. (94 words) 472

The inevitable delays there, due to his late arrival and apparent 538
discontinuance of issuing visas for the day, meant that Mr Connell did not 614
leave the embassy premises until 1800 hours. He then encountered the rush- 690
hour traffic, and finally reached Heathrow Airport at 1930 hours. Having 766
parked his car in the long-stay uncovered car park he checked into the 836
hotel, fortunately very conveniently situated for the airport terminal 906
buildings, and arranged an early morning call for 0530 hours. However, the 982
room allocated was badly positioned both with regard to noise from within 1055
the hotel and the sound of aircraft landings and takeoffs. Mr Connell had 1131
little sleep. (229 words) 1144

At 0615 the following day, he transferred to the airport via the hotel 1215
courtesy bus. Having then collected the necessary tickets from the Iraqi 1290
Airways desk, and weighed in the luggage (which incurred an excess baggage 1366
charge as it was 8 kg over the 20 kg allowance), he settled down in the 1438
lounge of Terminal 3 to wait for the flight to be called. In the event, 1512
there was a 5-hour delay for which no proper explanation was given, but Mr 1587
Connell occupied himself by reading 'The Times', browsing through a leaflet 1667
which Clare had photocopied on 'Muslim Social Customs', and putting on to 1746
dictaphone much of the outstanding correspondence awaiting his attention. 1819
The airline provided complimentary vouchers for lunch by way of 1883
compensation for the flight delay, and the aircraft finally departed at 1954
1310 hours. (393 words) 1965

(Extract from *Case Study Assignments in Secretarial Procedures*, Joanna Gaukroger, McGraw-Hill, 1986.)

10 mins

address in Data Files, filename ALPHA, page 102

(5) Letter to Applied Technology Inc f ao Michael Jones

Mark URGENT

Dear Sirs, Further to our / recent telephone conversation, I enclose 3 copies of our reply to yr invitation to tender dated 31/3.

We have included a full range of sample reports for the / stock management system, altho' I am aware that you may already have rec'd the drafts from Nigel Travers. [I look forward to seeing you again on (typist check date from itinerary). Y f.

in top r-h corner please mark in CAPS BRING FORWARD (enter date as 1 calendar month from today)

35 mins

(6)

Table 1.1 Office printers–comparative features ← Emphasize Heading

Type	Speed	Main uses	Advantages	Disadvantages
Daisywheel	Up to 70 cps	WP, electronic typewriters	Top quality print, changeable printwheels	Relatively expensive to buy and run, limited to the characters on the available printwheels, noisy, slow
Dot matrix	200 cps, up to ~~100~~ 1000 in nlq	Drafts, nlq for WP, home computers, some graphics	Cheap to buy and run, wide range of ~~possible~~ characters/colours available	Printing in nlq can be ~~very~~ slow on cheaper models, not suitable for ~~top~~ better quality output, noisy
Ink jet	Up to 4/5 pages a minute, (nlq slower)	Some WP, OHPs, charts, graphs and diagrams, when colour is required	Flexibility, use of colour, quiet	More expensive than ~~dot~~ LETTER matrix, no multiple copies, special paper often required to produce quality results
Laser	Up to an A4 page in 6 seconds	All, but particularly DTP ~~desktop publishing~~ and WP	Flexibility, good quality / quiet output	No multiple copies, can be expensive to run, ~~expensive~~ & to buy

cps = charactes per second dtp = desk top publishing ~~WP = word processing~~ nlq = near letter quality.

rule between columns

Type word processing in full throughout

TIMED SKILL MEASUREMENT 4

keystrokes

Although seals are regarded by Scottish lairds and anglers as predators of 76
wild salmon, and as such are classed as vermin (along with foxes and rats) 152
the nation as a whole appears to view them in a similar light to household 226
pets - leaping to their defence in the face of adversity. (56 words) 283

For many, the exciting news is that seals have recently been spotted 352
swimming in The Thames - and not just around the estuary. A few years ago, 430
a seal was spotted as far up as Teddington Weir, on London's south-west 505
edge, and sightings of seals by regular river users are becoming much more 579
frequent. (117 words) 588

Those in The Thames are common seals, Phoca vitulina - smaller than the 663
more publicized grey seal (which is concentrated around Scottish coastal 737
regions and islands). Apparently there is a small colony of common seals 812
living off the Essex sandbanks. This Essex colony produces a few pups each 890
year, which accounts for the increasing numbers seen up-river. Unlike the 965
grey seals, who spend the first few weeks of their life outside water, the 1039
common seal pups can swim within a few hours of birth - thus the Essex 1110
sandbanks can provide an adequate place for rearing the young seals. 1178
(235 words)

The much cleaner river water of the last few years has vastly increased the 1254
numbers of fish in The Thames, which is said to account for their 1321
appearance over the last few years. The presence of a few seals in rivers 1396
such as The Thames may indicate how resilient nature can be in the face of 1472
pollution, disturbance and habitat destruction. Alternatively, it may be 1546
taken as an indication of how, if we do continue to improve our 1609
environment, wildlife can and will return and flourish. Overall though, 1682
seals do seem happy enough to swim in some pretty dirty water - whether 1753
this will have any long-term effects on their health is as yet unknown. 1824
(364 words)

SKILL BUILDING 9

1 *Alphabetic sentences* Type each sentence twice.

To my amazement, the junior clerk learned the tasks and requested a promotion from the basic grade to a higher level with extra pay.

The expedition very quickly recognized it was hopeless in pitch black and stopped looking for the injured animal until the first sign of light.

2 *Correction of errors* Each sentence contains *at least* four word errors. Read each sentence, check spellings and then type each sentence correctly.

1 The companies policy is to allow 2 weeks anual leave during the Summer months' and one extra week during the off-peak season.

2 We have recently aquired a Liason Officer in our Welfare Department to assist staff whom have long term health problms.

3 Its often nesessary to seek an new appointment or an oportunity for promotion with company's other than this one.

3 *Improve control of hyphenated words*

profit-sharing short-term one-off one-way non-executive off-peak

high-flier price-sensitive tax-deductible re-entry day-to-day

loose-leaf, open-plan, cross-reference, earnings-related, up-to-date

4 *Skill measurement* Target time for each exercise is 1 minute, not more than 1 error.

With 4,500 employees in over 20 countries, Mexx Jackson Associates is undoubtedly one of the world's leading independent management and financial planning consultancies. TFRC, our marketing group, has recently completed assignments in Europe (Sweden and Luxembourg), Africa (Zambia and Ethiopia) and Asia (Pakistan and Malaysia).

340 keystrokes (68 words)

The biggest cause of time off work may not be what you'd expect. A new survey shows that the majority of the public expect it to be relatively minor ailments (colds and flu), backache - or at the other end of the spectrum union strikes and disputes. However, it's heart disease which keeps a quarter of a million people away from work each day.

340 keystrokes (68 words)

TIMED SKILL MEASUREMENT 3

keystrokes

Burford Foundries is a medium-sized Oxfordshire-based firm that supplies 75
engineering facilities on a turnkey basis to other countries. Its tender 149
to the Department of Supply of the Royal Government of Bruhal has enabled 227
the company to get on the initial shortlist of 6 companies for a multi- 297
million pound contract in Bruhal. (78 words) 331

Mr Nichols, the Sales Director of Burford Foundries, has flown Concorde to 412
the Kingdom in order to make a presentation of the company's case to the 486
Board of the Department of Supply. (104 words) 523

Mr Nichols made an excellent presentation, and despite the fierce 590
competition from German and Italian firms and from a Canadian company, he 666
feels confident that the contract will be theirs. (143 words) 715

The company's agent, however, has received a message from the Minister of 790
Supply. Burford Foundries must agree to pay 7% of the contract price to 866
the Minister after signing the contract if they wish to get the business. 941
(188 words)

This provides the Sales Director with several problems. Firstly, the 1014
original tender price was not inflated to allow for making extra payments 1087
to officials (known as 'introductory payments'). However, the agent has 1164
been informed that the Minister would allow an adjustment to the tender 1236
price for this purpose. Secondly, the payments would be, strictly 1303
speaking, illegal under UK law and the Sales Director wonders what his 1376
position would be when the company accounts come to be audited. Thirdly, 1450
the Director knows that if Burford won the contract, 350 extra jobs would 1525
be created for the firm over the next two years and the company itself 1595
would receive international recognition. If he refuses to make the extra 1669
payments, the business is thought likely to go to a German firm, Burford 1743
Foundries' major competitor. (354 words) 1773

Exercise 1

Type the following organization chart on A5 landscape paper. Use margins of 12 pitch 22–78. Rule as shown.

```
Chairman      Turn up 2 linespaces
|
Managing Director    Turn up 1 to the horizontal line and 2 afterwards
|
+----------+-----------+------------+----------+
|          |           |            |          |
Chief      Company     Chief        Projects   Marketing
Engineer   Secretary   Accountant   Manager    Manager
```

Exercise 2

Type the following organization chart on A5 landscape paper. Centre the whole exercise across the page and rule as shown.

```
Managing Director    Turn up 1 linespace
|
+---------------------+------------------------------+
|                     |                              |
Production Director   Administration Manager         Chief
|                     |                              Accountant
+--------+            +----------+
|        |            |          |
Design   Production   Personnel  General Services
                      Officer    Manager
```

Exercise 3

Type the following organization chart on A5 landscape paper. Centre the whole exercise across the page and rule as shown.

```
                  +-- Technical Officer
                  |
                  +-- Finance Officer
                  |
                  +-- Administration Officer
Chief             |
Executive    -----+
                  +-- Planning Officer
                  |
                  +-- Housing Officer
                  |
                  +-- Education Officer
```

TIMED SKILL MEASUREMENT 2

keystrokes

Les Bastides Blanches was a village of 150 inhabitants, perched on the prow 78
of one of the last foothills of the Massif de L'Etoile, about 10 kilometres 156
from Aubagne. A dirt road led there on a slope so abrupt that from afar it 233
appeared to be vertical; on the hillside beyond, nothing but a mule track 306
left the village, with a number of footpaths leading off it to the sky. 377
(75 words)

About 50 rows of houses, whose whiteness remained only in the village's 450
name, line 5 or 6 streets that were neither paved nor tarred - streets that 525
were narrow because of the sun and tortuous because of the mistral. 592
(118 words)

There was however a fairly long esplanade that dominated the valley on the 667
west; it was supported by a rampart of trimmed stone a good 10 metres high, 742
finished off with a parapet under a row of ancient plane trees. The place 817
was called the Boulevard, and the old people came there to sit and talk in 892
the shade. (180 words) 902

In the middle of the Boulevard a very wide flight of a dozen steps rose to 978
the town square bordered by facades around a fountain with a stone shell 1050
attached to the middle. This was the origin of the village. Fifty years 1125
earlier, a summer resident in Marseille (2 or 3 would come during the 1196
hunting season) had left a small bag of coins to the community, and this 1271
had made it possible to conduct sparkling water from the only important 1342
spring in this part of the country to the square. It was then that the 1414
small farms scattered about the valleys and hillsides had been abandoned 1486
one by one, and the families had grouped themselves around the fountain, 1558
and the hamlet had become a village. (318 words) 1594

All day long one saw pitchers or jars under the jet of water and gossips 1667
listening to their rising music while they exchanged news of the day. 1736
(347 words)

(Extract from *Jean de Florette* by Marcel Pagnol—English version published by Andre Deutsch, 1988.)

Exercise 4

Type the following centred organization chart on A5 paper.

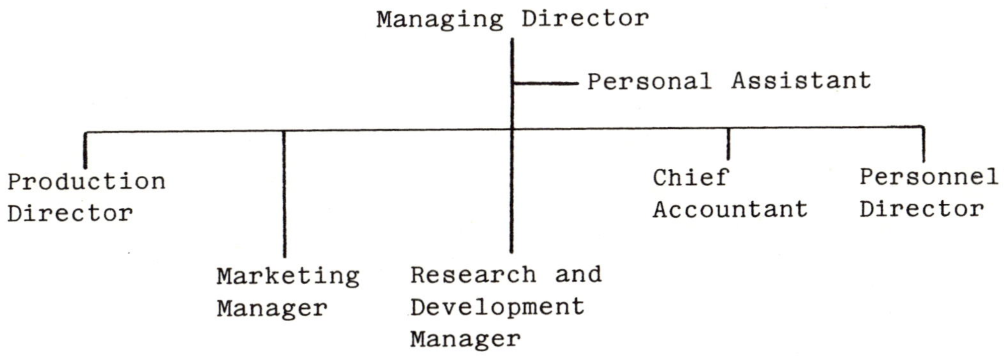

Exercise 5

Type the following centred organization chart on A5 paper.

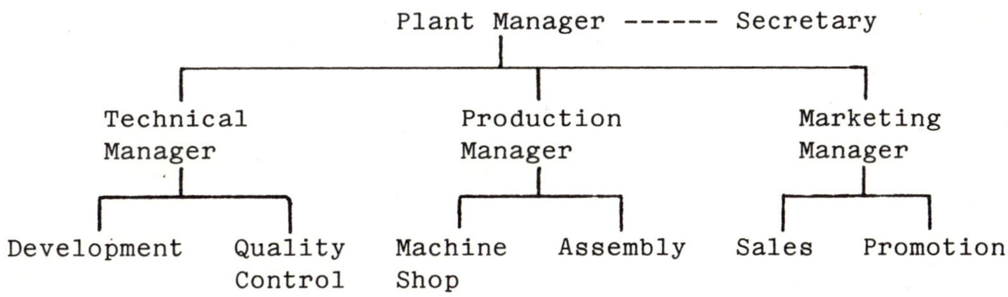

Exercise 6

Type the following chart on A4 portrait paper.

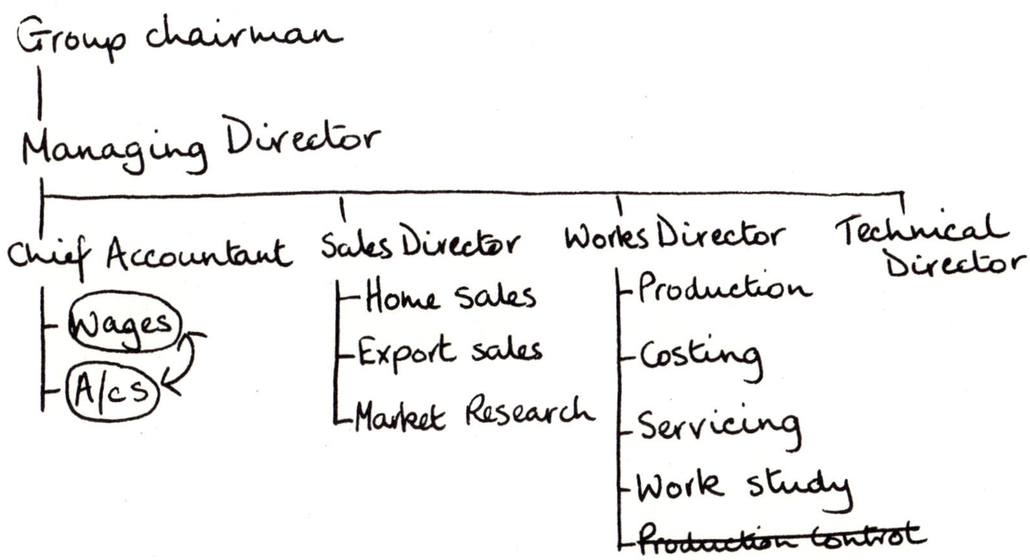

TIMED SKILL MEASUREMENT 1

keystrokes

A recent business lunch in the Polish restaurant off Crompton Street says 76
all. (16 words) 80

The surroundings are far from elegant - shiny black tables, covered in 151
faint scratches, and hard ladder-back chairs - around and on which our party 227
of 4 was squashed quite uncomfortably. The noise from the adjacent 295
champagne and vodka bar rendered conversation of the most primitive type 367
virtually impossible. (77 words) 388

The menu is short, with many of the dishes crossed out or overwritten in 461
such a way as to make the whole thing quite illegible - better to ask the 534
waiter - who speaks excellent English with only the faintest trace of an 607
accent. He will attempt to pronounce the impossible and identify the range 683
of potential ingredients - constantly slipping in the importance of 750
ordering drinks from the restaurant's internationally acclaimed choice of 824
14 different vodkas. (168 words) 844

Our aperitif was Krupnik, a deliciously-hot blend of honey, spices and 916
vodka. To start the meal, my companions feasted on plates of tasty, if 988
somewhat salty, herring fillets with boiled potatoes - I selected a bowl of 1064
above-average bortsch. Our main courses were less successful - avoid the 1138
boiled chicken - patrons from the next table even complained that theirs 1210
was inedible! Bigos, the Polish national dish of sauerkraut and mixed 1283
meats, well-flavoured with juniper, lacked its usual robust flavour; only 1356
the Warsaw steak, thick cut and with a mound of fried onions seemed to live 1432
up to the promise of the bortsch. (292 words) 1465

To follow? Poppy seed cakes, blinis and strong black coffee. Avoid the 1541
wines - there is nothing unusual, and most are over-priced - too many 1610
rounds of vodka and the ill-fated Krupnik brought our bill to £110 for 4! 1686
(336 words)

Exercise 7

Type the following chart on A5 landscape paper. Keep all the boxes the same size and leave five character spaces to the left and right of the centre box.

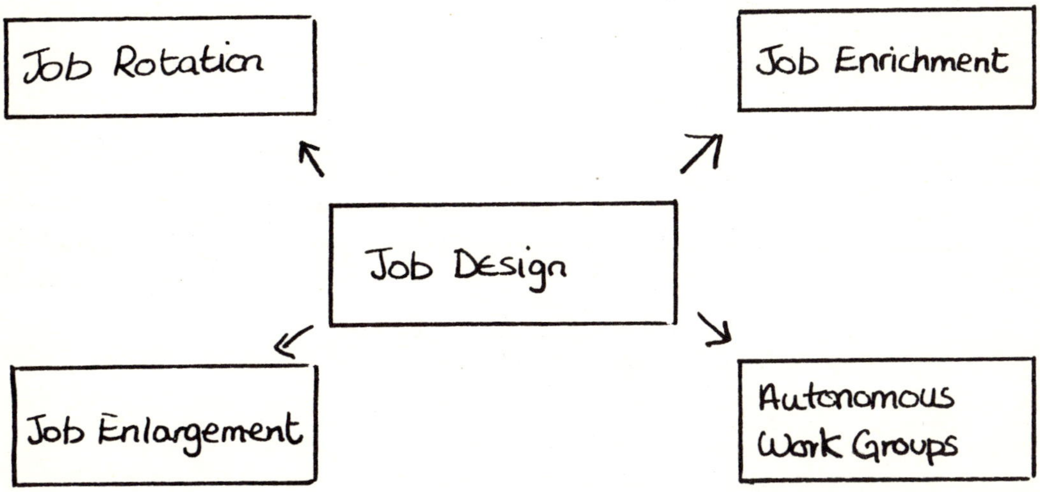

Key in exercise 7 (filename BOXES) for 10-pitch printout. Use the save function for the first box and then copy and insert at the appropriate places. When you have completed this task, save under filename BOXES. Retrieve the document and follow instructions for text editing on page 100.

Exercise 8

Type the following chart on A5 paper. Each square should be 10 linespaces in depth.

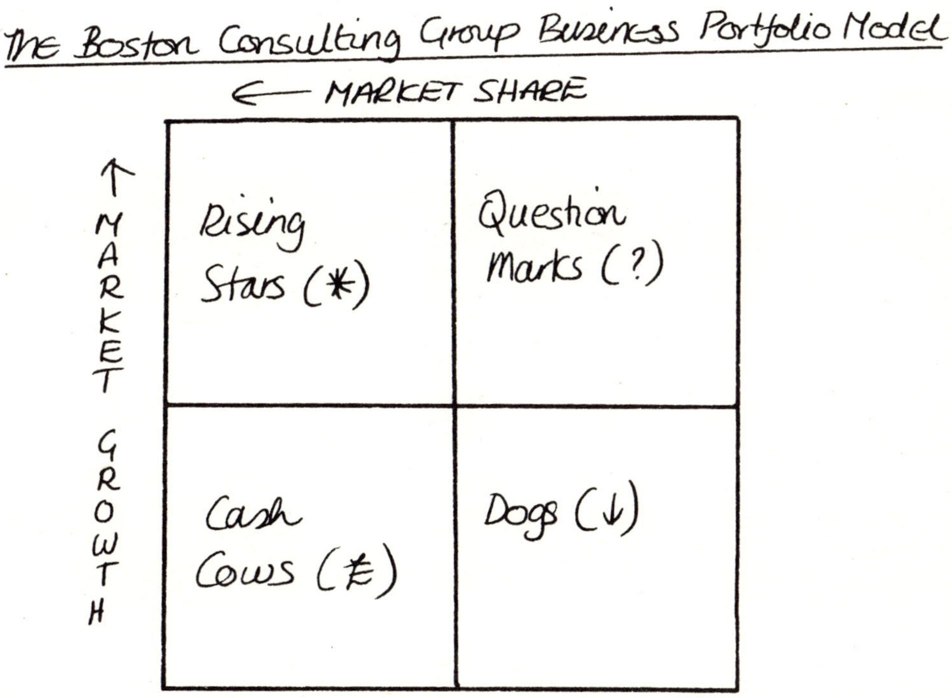

6

15 mins

DIRECTIONS

~~LOCATION MAP~~

(from Liverpool St

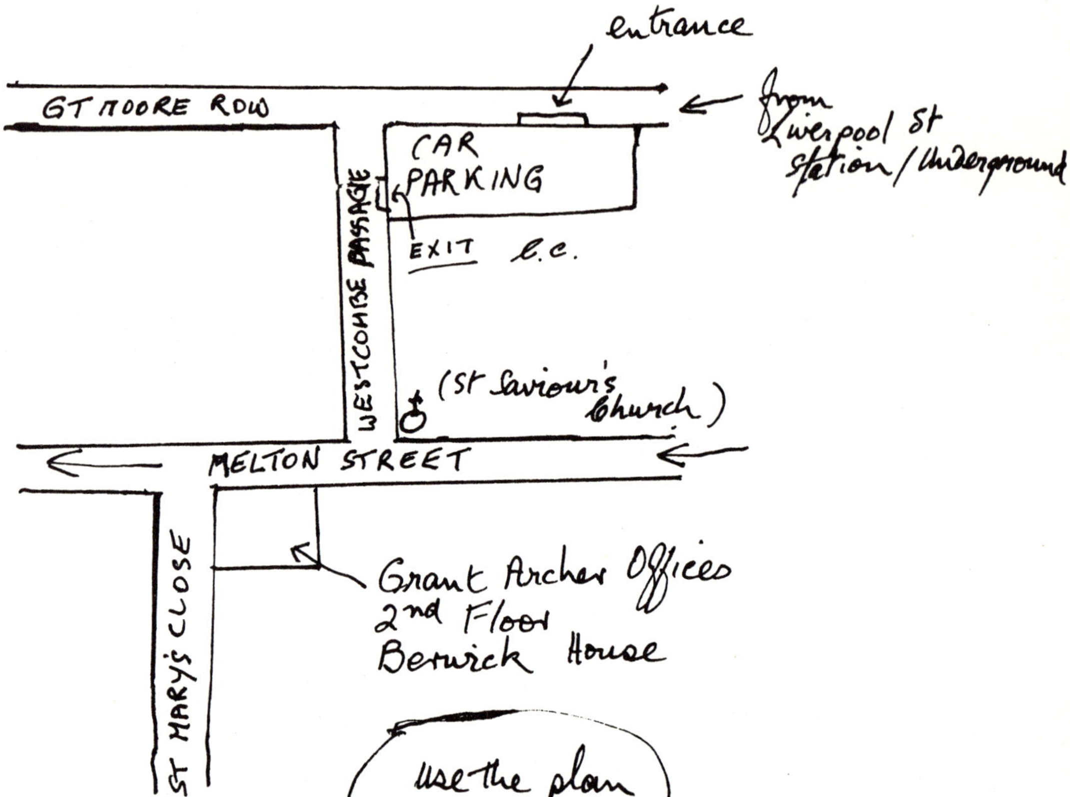

Use the plan provided*

* See **Workguide and Resource Material**

Exercise 9

Type the following chart on A5 landscape paper.

PRODUCTION & INTERNATIONAL TRADE FLOWS OF CARS (1986)

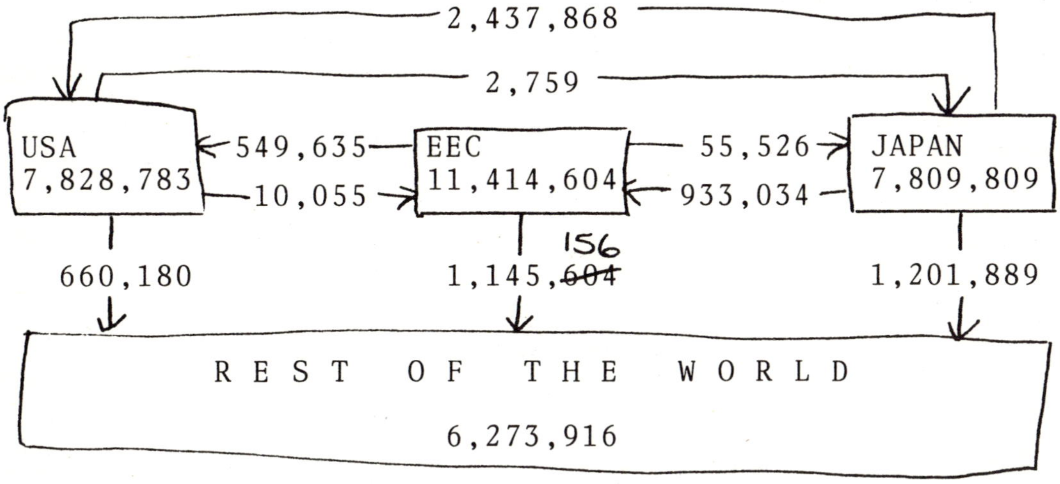

Source: Verband der Automobilindustrie eV, Tatsachen und Zahlen aus der Kraftverkehrswirtschaft (1987)

Exercise 10

Type the following chart on A5 landscape paper.

INTERNATIONAL DIALLING TO THE USA

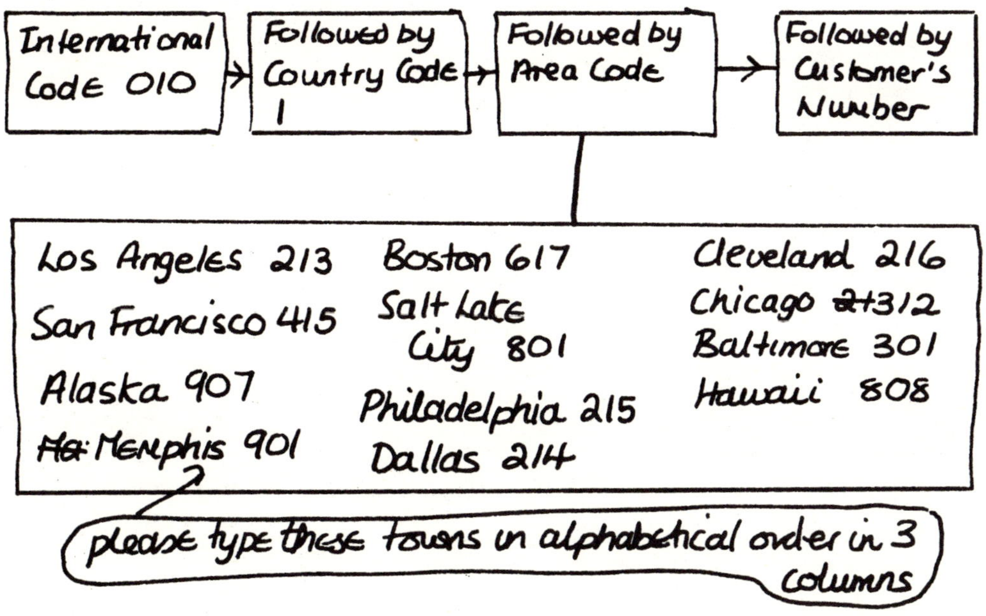

3.3. Local Labour Market Survey

The report suggests th after 1994 the no of local 16-yr-old school leavers rises again. W the local economy in a strong position, a no of families are ~~beginning~~ starting to move into the area.

4 Recommendations

4.1. The Manpower Planning Cttee consider as a matter of urgency:

4.1.1. the current career structure for Sec staff & the poss of upgrading senior sec staff to reflect the resp of their positions.

4.1.~~2~~3 Liason with the Public Relations Cttee to discuss what opps exist for improving our image locally (eg appealing to women returners)

4.1.~~3~~2 a range of short-term incentives wh might encourage & retain quality clerical & sec staff.

5 Conclusion

~~Their is evidence to suggest th we are not currently attracting candidates of the right calibre for sec posts.~~

~~Action must be taken~~ quickly ~~if we are to prevent~~ more ~~serious recruitment problems over the next few years~~

-- ooOoo --

Typist — please type in double spacing - number pages centre bottom and type draft in top r-h corner of each page.
All ~~main~~ the 5 report headings in closed caps. Please inset each sub-paragraph - eg

2
 2.1
  2.1.1
  2.1.2

Exercise 11

Type the following diagram on A5 landscape paper.

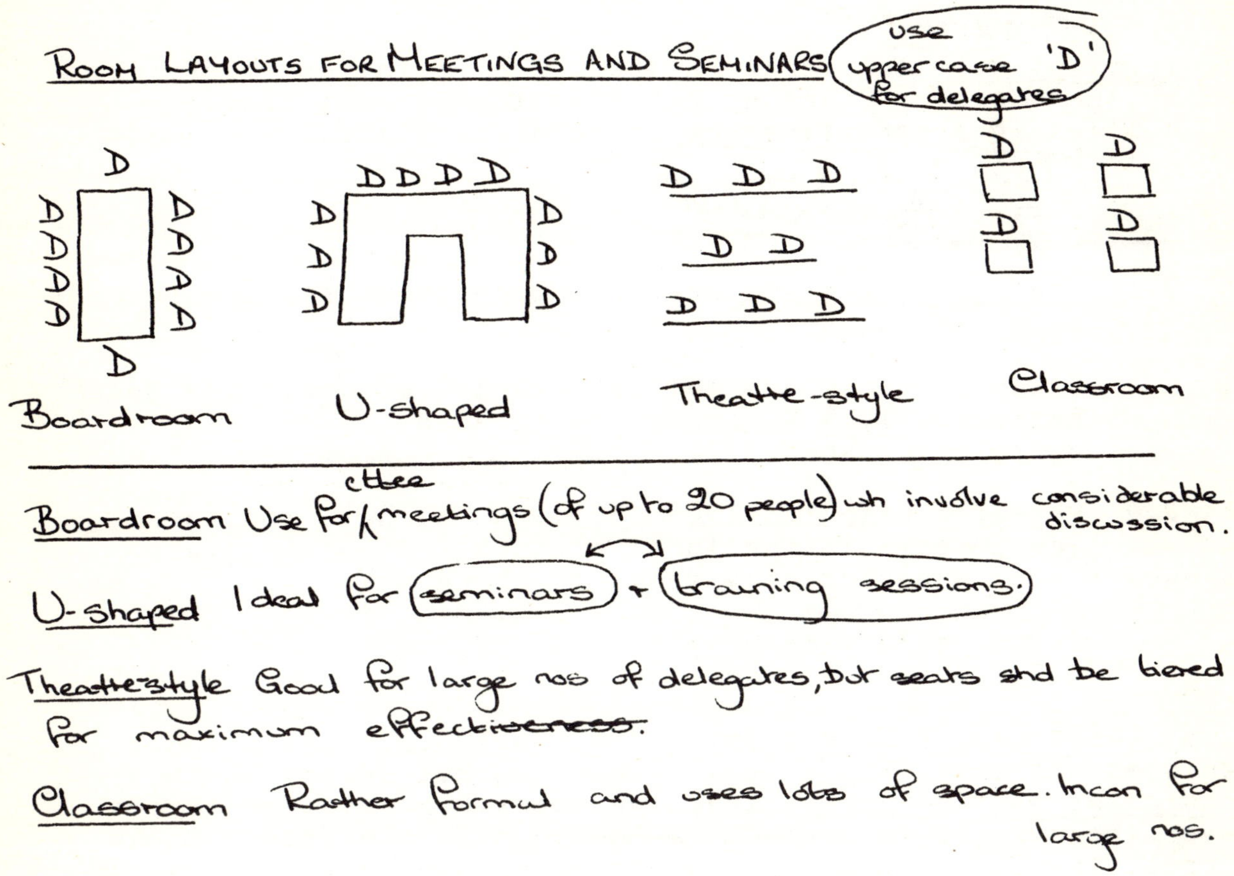

Exercise 12

Type the following diagram on A5 portrait paper.

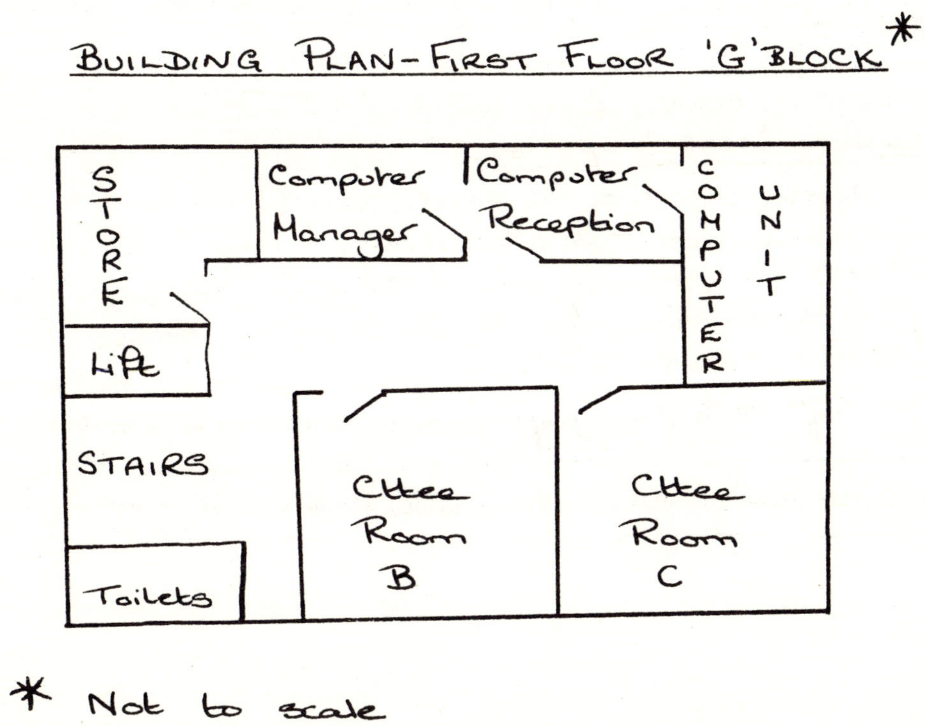

5 (35 mins)

Manpower Planning Review – Secretarial recruitment ← CLOSED CAPS

(closed caps)

1 Terms of Ref To prepare a short report for consideration by the Manpower Planning Cttee on the current difficulties in precruiting new secretarial staff. Submission date ← (first Tuesday of next mth – typist pse insert date)

2 INVESTIGATYIONS

2.1 Staff Interviews Personel Department staff have interviewed:

2 senior secs/personel assistants (graded above 4), 2 4 secs (grded 3/4), 4 WP operators (graded 2), 4 junior WP operators graded 1/2). / clerical assistants — list these

2.2 Research with local competitors We have monitored job adverts in the local press & approached staff agencies over a period of 4 weeks to check on:

2.2.1 salary levels;
2.2.2 terms & conditions of work.

2.3 Local Labour Market Info The County Council is in ~~ht~~ the eprocess of compiling a local labour market survey which indicates shortage areas, training needs & population trneds over the next (5) 10-yr period. ~~S Howell~~ Louise Beckwith has interviewed Brian Jones, the County Council Project Supervisor.

3 FINDINGS

Staff Interviews

3.1 Employees have made the following observations:

3.1.1. promotion for good (junior) staff within our org is limited;
3.1.3 holiday entitlement, hrs of wk & facilities are considered to be adequate;
3.1.2 our training programme is considered to be 1 of the best in the area
3.1.4 Salaries at WP operator level are good, (insert a)

3.2 Research w Local Competitors

3.2.1 Press advents suggest th the service sector (banking, building societies & insurance) offer better terms; mfring slightly less favourable terms. However, some ~~legal~~ service sectors (legal work & local authorities) offer sig lower salary levels.

3.2.2 Staff agencies report a decline of approx 50% since 1990 in the nos of enquiries from both young people & those returning to work.

(a but at senior levels compare unfavourably w other local orgs)

Exercise 13

Type the following organization chart on A4 landscape paper.

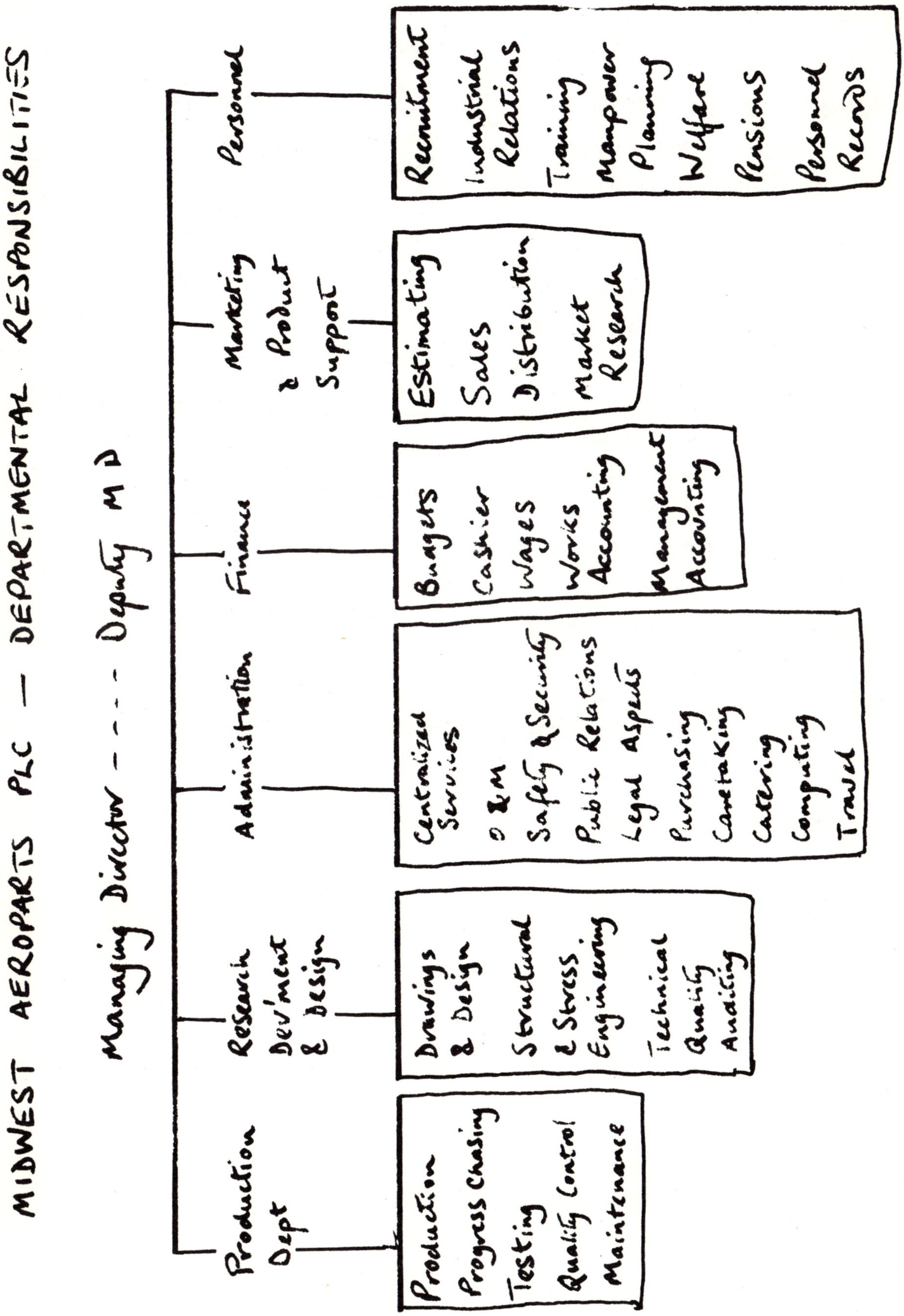

3 (25 mins)

Please prepare a standard letter to be sent to all job applicants informing them of interview arrangements.

~~Mark the letter 'Private'~~ use Ref PER/93/1, leave room for date + name & add (added later) Type first portion of salutation (Dear) subject heading: POST NO: (leave at least 10 spaces) JOB TITLE:

Thank them f their application. Say that our next selection day wl be on (leave about 2" for date) at our London offices. Map enclosed. Day starts about half 9 finishes before 4.30. Tell them to prepare the enclosed selection ex for presentation during the morning. Lunch provided.

(Shortlisted) candidates after the morning ex wl have a formal interview during the pm session – free to go after lunch if not shortlisted. Ask them to confirm acceptance by returning the slip below asap. Exps can be claimed on production of recs

ys

Jancis Owens (add designation + address)

Name ________

Address ________ etc

I confirm th I sh be attending the recruitment & selection ex on (leave room for date).

Signed ____ Date ____

Exercise 14

Type the following chart on A4 plain paper. The top line of each box should be two character spaces to the right of the bottom line.

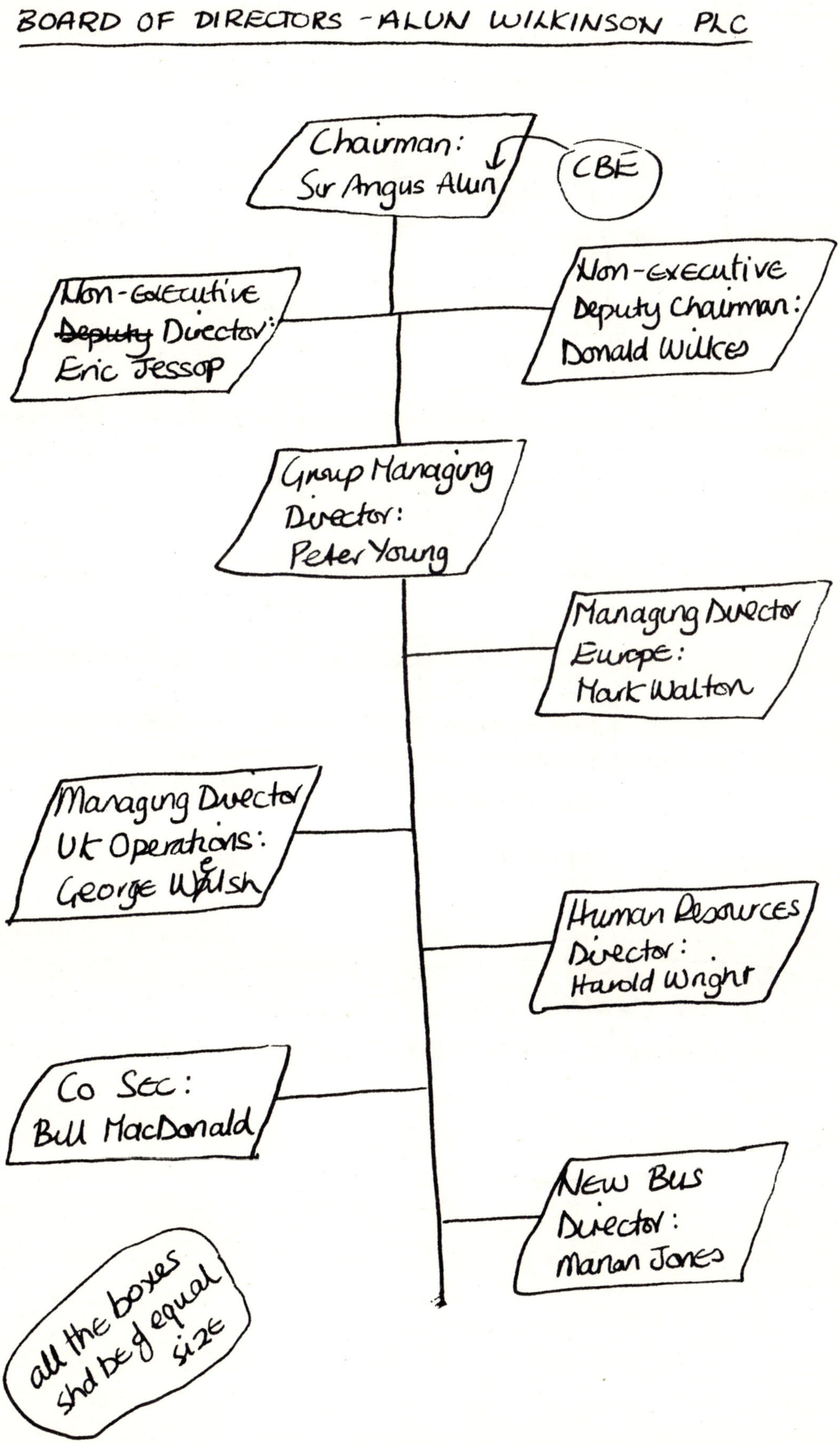

2 (15 mins)

GRANT ARCHER MANAGEMENT DEVELOPMENT AND TRAINING

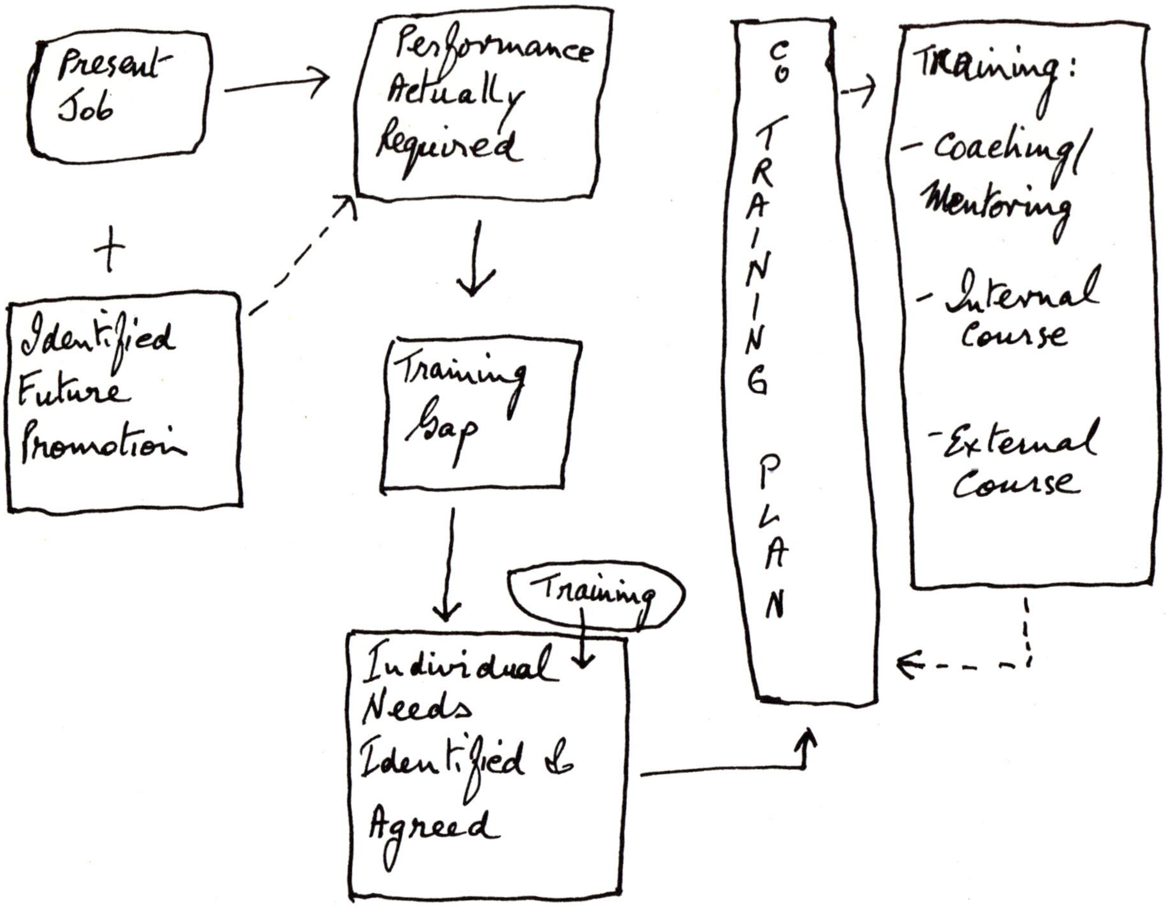

please use capital letters throughout.
Leave at least 1" (26 mm) between each of the 4 columns

Exercise 15

Type the following decision tree on A4 landscape paper. Draw all the lines before beginning to type.

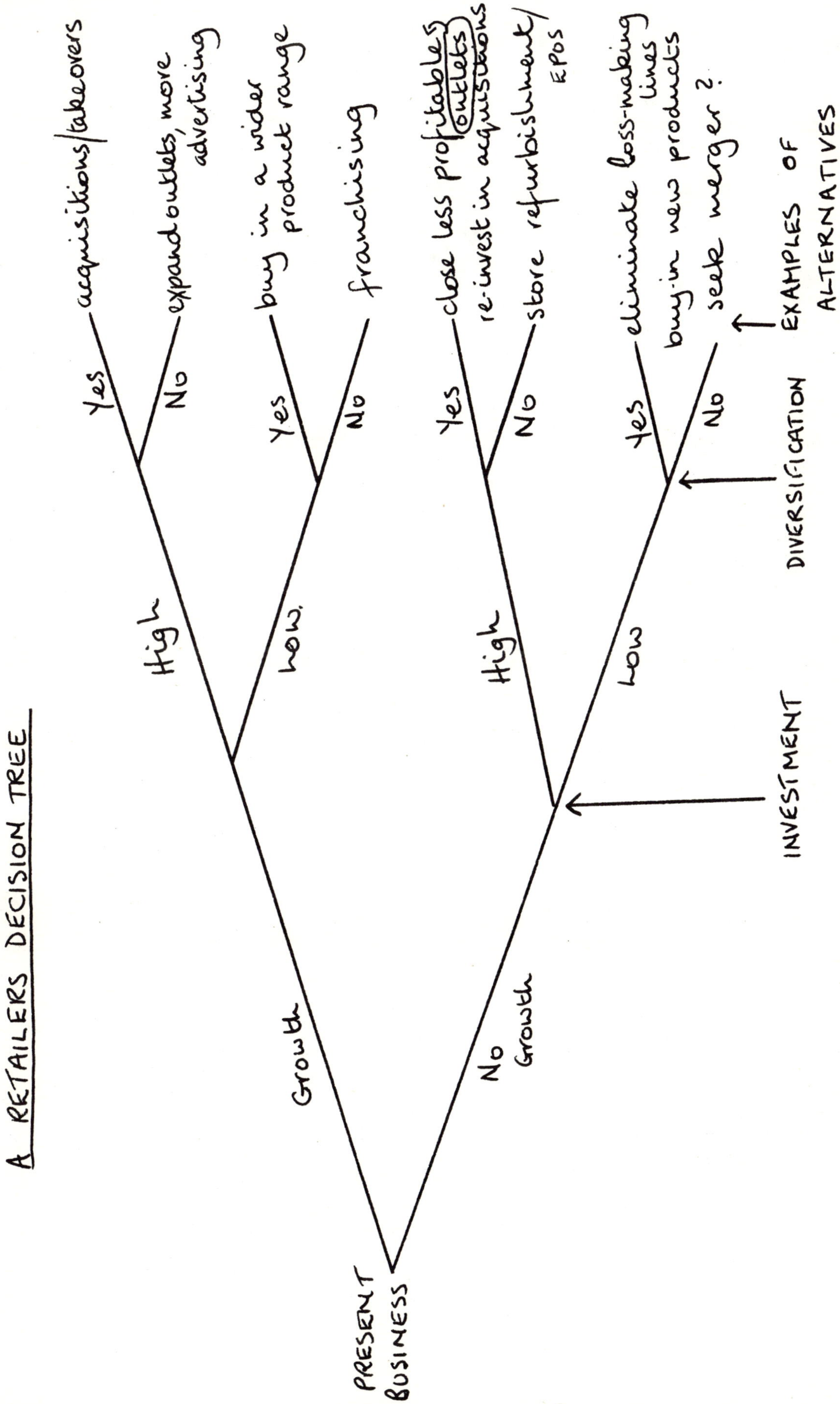

1 (35 mins)

Typist – on 2 pages – Second page to start after lunch

GRADUATE SELECTION PROGRAMME FOR MANAGEMENT TRAINEES

PART A PRESENTATION EX

8.45
Meeting of staff participants in Cttee Room A
9.00

	NAME	WAITING ROOM	INTERVIEW ROOM	STAFF PARTICIPANTS
9.00 – 9.25	MAUREEN Sheila O'Farrell	Cttee Rm C	Cttee Rm A	
9.30 – 9.55	Siân Joanne Nash			Richard Winter Jancis Owens
10.00 – 10.25	Sharon Jane Walter			Richard Morrison Robert Porter
10.30 – 10.55	David John Lewis			
11.00 – 11.25	Timothy ~~Pete~~ Jonathan Harvey			

List down the columns in alphabetical order lc

11.30 – 12.00 Meeting of staff participants to make their short-listing decisions

12.00 – 12.15 Communication of shortlisting decisions – all candidates to be in Cttee Rm C.

12.15 – 1.00 LUNCH

Caps Part B INTERVIEW

1.15 – 1.15 Pre-interview meeting of the panel.

		Cttee Rm C	Cttee Rm F	
1.15 – 2.15				
2.15 – 3.15				
3.15 – 4.15				Jancis Owens Richard Morrison Nigel Travers
4.15 – 5.15				

alphabetically as above

Repeat headings: (1) Waiting Rm (2) Interview Rm (3) Staff Participants

5.15 – 6.00 Private Meeting of the interview panel lc

SKILL BUILDING 10

1 *Alphabetic sentences* Type each sentence twice.

Both clerks were given expensive quartz watches to commemorate the anniversary of their joining the department.

Typing a boxed table with just horizontal headings is far quicker and simpler than vertical or diagonal ones.

2 *Correction of errors* Each sentence contains *at least* five word errors. Read each sentence carefully and then type each sentence correctly.

1 In the absense of our assistant, thankyou for arranging the accomodation for the Chairman's Advisery Comittee so promtly.

2 The ammount of stationary used in the buisness has increased dramatically over recent weeks, and is now considerable in exess of the alocated budget.

3 Unecessary though it may seem, we have refered the desision on this ocasion to a competent independant consultant.

3 *Practise typing telephone code numbers*

Germany (Berlin) 010 49 30

Japan (Tokyo) 010 81 3

USSR (Moscow) 010 7 095

China (Beijing) 010 86 1

Italy (Rome) 010 39 6

Spain (Madrid) 010 34 1

Brazil (Ribeirao Preto) 010 55 16

Egypt (Port Said) 010 20 66

4 *Production development from manuscript*

Reading time: 1 minute Target typing time: 2 minutes

Leroy Young, who earlier this yr took over from his father as head of Leisure Plus 99 plc, gave us good reasons why he decided to dispose of 1 particular hotel & ~~recreational complex in Yorkshire~~. [Leroy (28) has shown his determination to rid the group of all unprofitable enterprises & upgrade the portfolio to capture the bus user. The hotel in question ~~was the Queens just outside Sheffield~~. Altho' sited in the High Peak, the location ~~is distinctly~~ was off-centre for his target market. [' No one could find it. I spent ~~3~~ 4 yrs at Sheffield University & I couldn't track it down,' he admitted, ' It had to go!' (attractively)

600 keystrokes (120 words)

GRANT ARCHER & ASSOCIATES

OFFICE SERVICES – REQUEST FORM

This sheet contains instructions that must be complied with when typing the documents. Read the information carefully before starting, and refer back to it frequently.

Typist's log sheet

Originator Jancis Owens   Department Personnel Manager   Date   Ext No 118

Typists operating a word processor, or electronic typewriter with appropriate function keys, should apply the following automatic facilities: top margin; carrier return; line-end hyphenation; underline OR bold print (embolden); error correction; centring; any other relevant applications.

Remember to (a) complete the details required at the bottom of the form; (b) enter typing time per document in the appropriate column; and (c) before submitting this **log sheet** and your completed work, enter TOTAL TYPING TIME in the last column so that the typist's time may be charged to the originator.

Document No	Type of document and instructions	Copies – Original plus	Input form¶	Typing time per document	Total typing time ¥
1	Interview Schedule	top copy only	~~ms~~ m/s		
2	~~Manga~~ Management Development and Training Chart	top copy only	m/s		
3	Form letter to interviewees	top copy +1	compose from notes		
4	Memo to Zoë Harris – I will let you have this as soon as it is finished.	top + 2	compose from notes	10 mins	
* 5	Manpower Planning Report – URGENT – please complete now	top copy +1	m/s		
6	Location Map – outline map enclosed	top copy only	m/s		
			TOTAL	TYPING TIME	

TYPIST – please complete:

Typist's name: Date received: Date completed:

Time received: Time completed:

If the typed documents cannot be returned within 24 hours, the office services supervisor should inform the originator. Any item that is urgent should be marked with an asterisk (*).

¶ T = Typescript   AT = Amended Typescript   MS = Manuscript   SD = Shorthand Dictation   AD = Audio Dictation

¥ To be charged to the originator's department.

Exercise 1

Type the following statement on A5 landscape paper.

valuation of raw materials (emphasize heading)

	FIFO*	£	LIFO**	£
March	2,000 @ £1	2,000	800 @ 90p	720
	400 @ 90p	360	1,600 @ £1	1,600
	2,400	2,360	2,400	2,320
May	400 @ 90p	360	400 @ £1.10	440
	200 @ £1.10	220	200 @ £1	200
	600	580	600	640
Remaining Stock	200 @ £1.10	220	200 @ £1	200

* FIFO = First In First Out
** LIFO = Last In First Out

Exercise 2

Type the following statement on A4 portrait paper.

SOURCES & APPLICATION OF FUNDS	£	£	£
Cash & short-term funds at start of yr			17,500
Sources of Funds			
Arising from Trading:			
Profit on ordinary activities before tax		175,000	~~220,000~~
Depreciation		50,000	~~225,000~~
			242,500
Application of Funds			
Payment of tax		[ ]	
Payment of dividends		[ ]	
Increase in Working Capital:			
Stock	25,000		
Debtors	45,000		
Trade creditors	(17,500)	[ ]	182,500
CASH & SHORT-TERM FUNDS AT END OF YR			60,000

(take these figures from DataFiles, filename FUNDS, page 103)

6 (35 mins)

G —— A —— & Associates

Expo Claims Form - Project Staff

(Asterisk the headings of - Overnight Accom, Subsistence Expo, Public Transport, Taxi Fares, & Other Expo.)

(Please add an extra column PUBLIC TRANSPORT* btwn Subsistence Expo & Taxi Fares.)

(Please type in capitals) → Please complete all sections & return to the Finance Office no later than 1st Thurs in ea mth.

Name . . . . Dept/Section . . . .

Mth End . . . . . Staff Grade . . . . . . Staff No . . . .

Location . . . . Car Registration No . . . Cubic Capacity (CC) . . .

Journey Ref No	Times of leaving & return	Mileage	Overnight Accom*	Subsistence Expo*	~~*~~Other Expo*	Taxi Fares*

(allow 6 sets of dotted lines)

* Please attach recs for all these items. Details of expo allowable for Project Staff are displayed on section noticeboards

Exercise 3

Type the following exercise on A4 Grant Archer headed paper (see *Workguide and Resource Material*).

(– CONSULTANT:)

FEES & EXPS APR 1991 ~~th~~ Jon Mandeville

MONTH END: APR 1991

(please check arithmetic)

(a) CLCS Pilot Project – 5 days agreed

5th Pilot Meeting in Salzburg
preparation of meeting paperwork
liaison with Martin Booth (CLCS)

	£
2 days' work @ £300 per day	600
Return fare to S____ (+ ~~day's~~ subsistence	290.45
Postage	3·24
Telephone	24·10
Photocopying (recs attached)	48·23
	775·72 ~~766·02~~

(Telex Costs £9·70)

(b) TACK Project – 8 days agreed

Presentation to TACK Management
preparation of final report
research into suppliers

4 days' work at £300 per day	1200
Return fare to Brighton (+ subsistence)	142.00
Fax charges (recs attached)	14·04
Overnight stay in Brighton	49·50
Photocopying (recs attached	15·48
	1421·02

(Plse note: fees include VAT at 15% VAT registration no 302 4385 399)

TOTAL AMOUNT NOW DUE £ ~~2387·04~~

Key in exercise 3 (filename FINAN) for 12-pitch printout. Embolden the main heading, use the automatic underline feature and the decimal tab key. When you have completed this task, save under filename FINAN. Recall the document and follow the instruction for text editing on page 100.

the front few carriages of our ~~train~~ finally arrived on the platform at V——, the guard suggested th those of us in the back portion who wished to get off could save some ~~time~~ mins by walking up through the train to the ~~front~~ ~~walking~~ station platform.

(front carriages of the)

This is not a letter complaining abt ~~the~~ regular breakdowns on the London u/ground service! ←

Several of my fellow passengers commented th they seemed to hv our interests at heart – a feeling wh seems to be increasingly rare – & for ~~this~~ alone they deserve to be congratulated.

(nowadays)

In fact, I shd like to recom the driver & guard for some sort of commendation.

5 (10 mins)

(BA FCA MBIM JP)

MARTIN FIELD WAS BORN IN ORFORD, SUFFOLK, & EDUCATED AT REPTON &

QUEENS' COLLEGE, OXFORD. AFTER OBTAINING AN UPPER-SECOND IN PSYCHOLOGY,

PARTNERS

HE TRAINED AS A CHARTERED ACCOUNTANT WITH HAROLD DREW & ~~CO~~ IN CAMBERLEY.

IN 1987 HE BECAME A CONSULTANT & LEAD A NO OF IMPORTANT PROJECTS FOR BLUE-CHIP COS IN THE AREA OF STRATEGIC CHANGE. MARTIN, WHO IS SINGLE, LIVES IN WINCHCOMBE, GLOUCESTERSHIRE. HE JOINED GRANT ARCHER AS A SENIOR CONSULTANT & WAS APOINTED MD IN 1990.

(in 1985)

Please type on a postcard using lower-case letters & initial capitals as appropriate

Exercise 4

Type the following on A4 plain paper.

INVESTMENTS

Principle Associated Cos & other trade investments	Issued Share Capital	
	Total	Group Percentage
1.1. In Australia	A$	
Ausfields Pty Ltd	2,000,000	50
1.2 In England	£	
Rosford PLC	47,900,340	23.74
3½% Preference Shares	75,000	–
5¼% " "	75,000	–
1.3 In New Zealand	NZ$	
F W Industries Pty Ltd	42,140	25.4
1.5 In W Germany	DM	
Deutscher Supermarkt GmbH	56,444,000	45
8% Preference Shares	5,000,000	–
1.4 In USA	$	
W Wrag Adhesives Corporation	12,440	50

Notes:

1. There is no loan capital in any of the cos.
2. The reserves of Rosford PLC at 30 Sept amounted to £550 million.
3. The reserves of Deutscher S—— G—— at 31 Dec amounted to DM 83 million.

Key in exercise 4 (filename SHARE) for 10-pitch printout. Use the automatic underline for *Principal Associated*, etc, and for the numbered headings, the save function for the first horizontal line and copy where necessary, and the vertical line key for the vertical lines. When you have completed this task, save under filename SHARE. Recall the document and follow the instructions for text editing on page 100.

Use 24-hour clock

4 30 mins address in Data Files, filename ALPHA, page 102.

f a o The Chairman

Subject heading: London Underground Circle Service

My train this morning left Paddington at 8.58 & finally arrived at Victoria at 9.46. It had taken almost twice it's usual time to reach Victoria as there was apparently a technical failure at Notting Hill Gate wh was affecting all the network & causing chaos across a no of rush hr services. At ea station, where a few fellow passengers alighted, the platform was heaving w 100s of passengers desperately trying to board our train.

Our train was, by this time, over-full & it became increasingly hot & airless w the constant stopping, waiting & ~~restarting~~ starting again. The driver attempted to keep us relatively calm & cheerful by apologising for the delay, keeping & updating us every few mins on the latest position. The guard also did his best to control the hysteria wh followed our arrival at ea of the ~~other~~ stations intervening. ~~He shouted out the nature of the problem to the crowd, & assured the disappointed passengers th several other trains were following close behind.~~ When

us fully informed throughout the incident

of some sort

I am a ~~regular~~ frequent user of the circle line u/ground service fr Paddington Station to Victoria Station en route to our Central London & Bexley Heath offices.

Exercise 5

Type this vertical balance sheet on A4 paper. Follow the layout as indicated.

GROUP AND COMPANY BALANCE SHEETS

NET ASSETS	Group 31 May 1991 £000	Group 31 May 1990 £000
Fixed Assets		
Tangible Assets	297,407	213,719
Investments	3,370	5,599
Current Assets		
Stocks	175,715	156,112
Debtors	72,351	66,818
Investments	5,271	12,039
Cash at bank and in hand	38,701	14,989
Creditors:		
Amounts falling due within 1yr	<271,024>	<246509>
CAPS Net Current Assets	21014	3449
Total assets less current liabilities	332,791	222,767
Creditors:		
Amounts falling due after more than 1yr	<95,345>	<69,252>
Provisions for liabilities & charges	-	113
Minority interests	<1098>	<1204>
TOTAL NET ASSETS	226,348	152,434
Capital & Reserves		
Called up share capital	95446	94248
Share premium a/c	4237	3924
Revaluation reserve	51820	268
Profit & Loss a/c	74845	53984
TOTAL CAPITAL & RESERVES	226,348	142,424

Typist – Please change angular brackets to rounded brackets

Watch the national press for details of other venues.

G—— A—— was established in 1970 by Grant Young & Peter Archer in response to the needs of UK cos to hv access to superior independent managment consultancy expertise.

For further info contact: George Parkinson on (0451) 41047/8

ENDS

The bus now supports over 100 professional & clerical employees ~~in~~ & 25 consultants, & is regarded as 1 of the leading consultancies of its kind in Europe.

Change UK to British throughout

VENUES BOOKED SO FAR

Date	Town/City
14 July	Edinburgh
27 "	London
31 "	London
4 August	~~Leicester~~ London
12 August	Leicester
13 August	Leicester
27 August	Milton Keynes
1 September	Leeds
3 September	Leeds
9 September	Birmingham
12 September	Manchester

Exercise 6

Type the following consolidated profit and loss account on plain A4 paper. Follow the layout exactly. Use margins of 12 pitch 14–86 or 10 pitch 10–72.

DENES FASHIONS PLC

CONSOLIDATED PROFIT & LOSS ACCOUNT FOR THE YEAR ENDED 31 AUG 1991

Notes		1991	1990
		£000s	£000s
1	TURNOVER	190,021	146,045
	Cost of Sales	152,984	119,322
	Gross Profit	take from Data Files, filename FASH, page 103	
	Distribution Costs		
	Administrative Expenses	9,750	7,273
		21,763	16,013
	Share of Trading Loss of Associated Companies .	294	
1	Profits of Subsidiary Companies	7,044	4,740
	OPERATING PROFIT	28,513	20,753
2.	Net interest paid	854	690
	PROFIT ON ORDINARY ACTIVITIES BEFORE TAXATION	27659	20063
3.	Tax on profit on ordinary activities . .	9774	8271
	PROFIT ON ORDINARY ACTIVITIES AFTER TAXATION	17 885	11 792
4.	Extraordinary items after taxation	(563)	2147
	PROFIT FOR THE FINANCIAL YR . . .	17 322	13 939
	Dividends	11 524	5 117
	RETAINED PROFIT FOR THE YR . . .	5 798	8822
	EARNINGS PER SHARE	12.01p	8.73p

NOTES:

1. For breakdown please see page 4.
2. Loans, debentures, overdraft + freehold property.
3. Assumes Corporation Tax @ 37.9%.
4. Surplus on realization of property.

3 (25 mins) (Please adopt any suitable layout for press releases)

PRESS RELEASE

(Mark DRAFT)

CONSULTANCY SERVICES TO THE FASHION INDUSTRY

(Please add a note to George on the second + file copies: 'Please amend + despatch to papers & periodicals on database file FASH2')

On 25 Apr, G— A— wl be launching its European consultancy initiative. [Over the ~~last~~ past few yrs there hv been a no of gov-backed schemes designed to improve the quality & performance of UK enterprises via access to key consultancy services.]

Fr July to Sept, G— A— will be organizing low-cost, one-day seminars on 'Making Money in the European Fashion Market'. ←

The seminars wl provide key info on bus opps in France, Belgium, Spain, Luxembourg, Scandinavia, The Netherlands, Eire, ~~&~~ focusing particularly on the differing cultures + lifestyles of the population,

(This wl be a DTI-sponsored ~~event~~ initiative designed to help smaller fashion ~~manfrs + retailers~~ designers & mfrs profit fr entry into Europe.)

regional differences & economic trends. Follow-up services, tailored to yr individual needs & including the preparation of European Bus Plans by G— A— specialists can be discussed at ea seminar

Seminars booked so far include (typist - add these fr the table at the bottom of the next page)

SKILL BUILDING 11

1 *Alphabetic sentences* Type each sentence twice.

Our anxiety over his whereabouts was quite justified when he eventually turned up with a bruised chin, and grazed arms and knees.

The shops have bought a quantity of new jackets, in many sizes and styles, at extremely competitive prices.

2 *Practise typing foreign currency*

US dollars $450   Singapore Dollars S$240   Hong Kong Dollars HK$791

Australian Dollars A$131   French Francs FF28,000   Italian Lire L3,300

Danish Kroner DKr 25,000   Spanish Pesetas Pts 26,500

West German Deutschmarks DM 1300   New Zealand Dollars Z$332

3 *Practise typing in full punctuation* Type the following passage using full punctuation.

Mr P G Bosonnet MA (Oxon) and Mr C A P Foxall BA, were appointed to the Board on 23 June 1989 and 1 July 1989 respectively. BHD Enterprise Co Ltd has also announced the appointments of Dr D Vander Warr and Mr G T McLaren as non-executive directors with effect from 1 December 1989.

4 *Skill measurement* Target time for each exercise is 1 minute, not more than 1 error.

In an unprecedented court action a British Rail station announcement system, accused of being too loud and clear, has been banned by local magistrates. Residents were driven to despair by the plummy strident tones echoing throughout the day and night, disturbing their sleep and shattering the peace of the surrounding countryside. They christened the voice 'Her Ladyship'.

370 keystrokes (74 words)

Voted first again in catering by all trade show exhibitors! Established in 1969, we pride ourselves in being able to offer a unique combination of personal service coupled with a high level of expertise. For top-quality hot and cold buffets, whether for the Director's Dining Room, informal entertaining or a celebratory lunch, you can be sure of a competitive quotation.

370 keystrokes (74 words)

2 (20 mins)

Champagne Reception Dinner Thurs 26 Apr 1991 Menu Selections

English	French	German	Italian
Salad of smoked l.c. Salmon ~~strip~~ strips	Effilochées de saumon fumé~~t~~ en salade	Salat mit geräuchertem Lachs	Insalata con salmone affumicato
Rump steak w Bearnaise sauce	Coeur de Rumsteack Bérnaise	Rumpsteak mit Bernaise - Soße	Rumpsteak salsa Bearnaise
John Dory fillet w tarragon	Blanc de St-Pierre à l'Estragon	Peterfischfilet mit Estragon	Filetto di pesce San Pietro al estrangone
Selection of desserts	Valse des desserts	Verschiedene Desserts ~~&~~ ~~zur~~ ZUR ↑ Auswahl	Vari desserts a scelta

Please rule as appropriate

Exercise 1

Type the following quick reference guide on A4 paper. Do not number or date the second page.

WORDPOWER QUICK REF GUIDE

F1 FORMAT MENU I - margins, tabs (left, right, centre, decimal), character pitch & justification

ALT + F1 DISC CHANGE - use this ~~to~~ when you change yr working disc

F2 SUPERSCRIPTS/SUBSCRIPTS — (eg H_2O, m^2)

F2 + ALT (format menu II) - line spacing emboldening & underscore

F3 (Alternative Characters) - changing the keyboard to accom foreign characters, mathematical & scientific symbols (eg é ñ ≡ ≤ √)

F3 + ALT PAGINATION - automatic pagination, manual page breaks, page formatting & 'keep' facility, page numbering

F4 PRINT MENU - nos of copies, cut/continuous feed, single pages or full docs

F5 IMPORTING TEXT - inserting another doc into the 1 already on screen

ALT + F4 STOP PRINTER

F5 + ALT CENTRING TEXT

F6 (Block menu) (cut/paste & boilerplating) - marking, moving & deleting blocks of text

F6 + ALT (Showing codes) - switching on codes

F7 (Spelling checker menu) - 50,000 word dictionery

ALT + F7 GOTO (menu) - top/bottom/left/right of current doc

F8

ALT + F8

F9

take from DataFiles, filename GUIDE, page 103

please draw a square around all keys (ALT and the F numbers) when you have finished

F9 + ALT AUTOMATIC INDENT MENU

F10 (Headers & Footers) - repeat headings & footnotes on docs

ALT + F10 ARITHMETIC MENU - checking docs (+ - x ÷)

change spelling of disc to disk throughout; type 'doc' in full; type circled items in closed capitals

Key in exercise 1 (filename GUIDE) for 12-pitch printout. Automatically underline all the words to be typed in closed capitals. When you have completed this task, save under filename GUIDE. Recall the document and follow the instructions for text editing on page 100.

GRANT ARCHER & ASSOCIATES

OFFICE SERVICES – REQUEST FORM

This sheet contains instructions that must be complied with when typing the documents. Read the information carefully before starting, and refer back to it frequently.

Typist's log sheet

Originator Martin Field Department Managing Director Date Ext No

Typists operating a word processor, or electronic typewriter with appropriate function keys, should apply the following automatic facilities: top margin; carrier return; line-end hyphenation; underline OR bold print (embolden); error correction; centring; any other relevant applications.

Remember to (a) complete the details required at the bottom of the form; (b) enter typing time per document in the appropriate column; and (c) before submitting this **log sheet** and your completed work, enter TOTAL TYPING TIME in the last column so that the typist's time may be charged to the originator.

Document No	Type of document and instructions	Copies – Original plus	Input form¶	Typing time per document	Total typing timeҰ
1	Memo to Senior Consultants <u>Please type this as soon as it is ready</u>	Top + 1	M/S		
2	Table in 4 languages	Top + 1	M/S		
3	Press Release + envelope to George Parkinson	Top + 2	M/S		
4	Letter to London Transport + envelope	Top + 1	M/S		
* 5	Biographical details use A6 postcard + single spacing. <u>PLEASE TYPE NOW</u>	Top only	AT		
6	Expenses claim form for project staff	Top only	M/S		
			TOTAL	TYPING TIME	

TYPIST – please complete:

Typist's name:

Date received:
Time received:

Date completed:
Time completed:

If the typed documents cannot be returned within 24 hours, the office services supervisor should inform the originator. Any item that is urgent should be marked with an asterisk (*).

¶ T = Typescript AT = Amended Typescript MS = Manuscript SD = Shorthand Dictation AD = Audio Dictation
Ұ To be charged to the originator's department.

Exercise 2

Type the following check-list on A4 paper, repeating the main and column headings for page 2.

emphasize heading

CHECKLIST OF RESPONSIBILITIES - LEISURE AT WORK
Conference

TASK	RESPONSIBILITY	COMPLETED BY (DATE)
1) VENUE		
selection of venue in accordance with budget....................	PW	
clarification of requirements with venue, including catering, seating plans, signposting, security, audio-visual requirements, confirming nos & final arrangements...................	SL/ARP	
financial details w venue	PR	
2) Programme		
selection of & invitation to plenary session speakers	LW	
appt of workshop leaders	PR/LW	
drafting of final programme	SL	
printing of approved programme	SL	
clarification w speakers regarding fees & exps	ME	
3) Publicity		
design and preparation of publicity materials (advertising literature, logo, signs, advert design	ARP	
preparation of press release	PR	
selection of advertising media	ARP	

Please change ARP to AM throughout

SKILL BUILDING 12

1 *Alphabetic sentences* Type each sentence twice.

They booked an overnight sleeper from Monaco to Luxembourg and realized they quite enjoyed the new experience of travelling by train.

The major item taken on the agenda concerned our capacity to fulfil the requirements of the valuable Brazilian order without extra expense.

2 *Improve control of capital letters—Common abbreviations*

MBO = Management by Objectives; GNP = Gross National Product;

EEC = European Economic Community; HASAW = Health and Safety at Work

PhD = Doctor of Philosophy; CPU = Central Processing Unit

TA = Training Agency; MS-DOS = Microsoft Disk Operating System;

3 *Practise typing roman numerals*

I (1), V (5), X (10), L (50), C (100), D (500), M (1,000)

XV = 15, XL = 40, XLVIII = 48, LIX = 59, LXX = 70, XCVII = 97

XCL = 140, CLV = 155, CC = 200, CD = 400, DCXV = 615, DCCCLIX = 859

CM = 900, MCLVIII = 1,158, MDCCCL = 1,850, MMM = 3,000, CMMM = 2,900

4 *Production development from manuscript*

Reading time: 1 minute Target typing time: 2 minutes

~~Business~~ analysts were ~~furious~~ up in arms when Joe Nash announced th he was changing the cos yr-end from 31 Dec to 30 April – from there point of view it made it even more difficult to assess the cos future earnings. [1 reason given for this growing trend is the boom in ~~takeovers~~ Mergers & acquisitions. New yr-end dates need to be aligned with those of the new parent co. ~~Accountants~~ & Merchant bankers will ~~also~~ often advise ~~private~~ cos going to the Stock Market to adjust there yr-end to that of the rest of the sector – this helps analysts make performance comparisons.

650 keystrokes (130 words)

placing of adverts ARP

overseeing the direct mailshot LW

4) ADMINISTRATION

financial and budgetary control (including authorization & processing of all income & expenditure . . . . RAC

processing bookings by individuals & cos.... PW

duplication of speakers' notes & hotel details (including accom) . . . . RAC

operation of tel enquiry & booking services MR

Written confirmation of bookings MR

invoicing cos where nec MR

~~presp~~ preparation & despatch of joining instructions including travel ~~arrangements~~ details MR

printing of folders, badges, car parking permits, etc . . . . RC

please set this out as indicated overleaf – leave final column blank

Key in exercise 2 (filename CHECK) for 12-pitch printout. Embolden the numbered headings, use the repeater function for leader dots, the save function for the first horizontal line and copy this where necessary, and also use the vertical line key for the vertical lines. When you have completed this task, save under filename CHECK. Recall the document and follow the instructions for text editing on page 101.

ring is to be given, the bridegroom wl then be asked to place it on his bride's finger.

(3) Late arrival may mean th the marriage date or/time needs to be changed.

(d) Registration

The registration of yr marriage wl take place immed after the ceremony in the presense of all the witnesses.

When the entry has been made in the register the R—— ~~wl ask you whether all the particulars have been correctly recorded~~. BE SURE TO CHECK THIS CAREFULLY. (insert 1)

The R—— wl then call on you both & 2 witnesses to sign the entry. (insert 2)

The entire ~~cre~~ ceremony shd take about 20 mins.

(1) You may be put ~~to~~ to some inconvenience if errors discovered later have to be corrected.

(2) The bride shd sign in the name by wh she was known at the ~~then~~ time of the ceremony.

: — : — : — : — : — : ← (typist - add tailpiece)
— : — : — : — : —
: — : — : — : etc

Typist please note:
(1) all quotes shd be inset by 5 character spaces
(2) use /continued at the bottom of page 1

Key in exercise 5 (filename MARR) for 12-pitch printout. Embolden the lettered headings, (a), (b), etc, use the indent function/indent tab setting for the indented paragraphs and justify the right margin. When you have completed this task, save under filename MARR. Recall the document and follow instructions for text editing on page 101.

Exercise 3

Type the following cv, displaying each page as attractively as you can.

(spaced caps)

CURRICULUM VITAE

~~this to~~ (this is page 1 - centre each line horizontally & the whole page vertically)

David John Bryce
'Lansdowne'
Drovers' Road
Bridgnorth, Shropshire, WV16 4XY
Tel (0746) 992515
Date of Birth:
Marital Status:
Nationality:

(take from Data Files, filename VITAE, page 103)

(please type manager, management & programme in full throughout)

On Page 2

Education & Qualifications

1967-74 Tudor Grange Grammar Sch, Solihull
9 'O' level subjects, 3 'A's levels Pure Maths (B)
Geog (C)
Economics (C)

74-77 University of Aberystwyth
BA (Hons) Economics & Politics (2i)

1979-80 Preston Polytechnic, Lancashire
Graduate Diploma in Media & Journalism

Experience

77-78 ISI Plastics Division, Sheffield
~~Mgt Trainee - I spent & 12 mths on there graduate training prog gaining exp in the purchasing, accounting & export functions~~

(insert 1 from overleaf)

1983-86 Sports Presenter - Independent Radio News
Live coverage of a variety of national (and local) sporting events ~~& leisure~~
(including international football events, racing, showjumping,

Exercise 5

Type the following on plain A4 paper.

Yr Marriage

(a) Before the Wedding Day

The Superintendant Registrar's licence wl be required for yr marriage.

(b) On the Wedding Day

The time arranged for yr wedding is .... on .... [The bride & bridegroom shd arrive ~~15~~ 10 mins before the time indicated & must be punctual. [It is yr resp to provide at least 2 witnesses at yr marriage. (insert 3 from overleaf)

(c) The Ceremony

Before the ~~cre~~ ceremony begins the Registrar wl see you both, in private, to check all ~~the~~ particulars & collect (~~set~~ statutory) fees of £..... You wl each be asked yr name, address, age (marital status) & occupation & the name & occupation of yr father. [~~The cr ceremony wl be conducted by the Superintendent R—— or his/her deputy.~~

The introduction wl remind you of the solemn & binding character of the marriage ceremony. The Superintendent R—— wl ask each of you in turn to repeat:

'I do solemnly declare th I know ~~no~~ not of any lawful impediment why I (typist leave 25 c.s) .. may not be joined in matrimony to (leave 25 cs) ....'

You wl then ~~be called upon~~ join hands while each of you speaks the words by wh the contract of marriage is made, repeating after the S—— R——:

'I call upon these persons here present to witness th I (leave 25 cs) .. do take thee (leave 25 cs) .... to be my lawful wedded wife/husband.' [If a wedding

~~These notes~~ This leaflet wl help you. Please read it carefully & make sure th yr fiancé(e) also ~~understands~~ knows what is required.

& watersports. ~~Other items tested into local radio news slots~~

1986/7 Senior Presenter – RPM Radio Ltd – a regular afternoon slot on this ~~popular~~ local radio station, reporting & discussing a wide range of local & national current affairs, political debates [phone-ins] local & national celebrity interviews.

1987–9 Assistant to the General Mgr – RPM Radio Ltd – assisting the G— M— & on occasion his deputy, w budgeting, advertising, staffing, & the general day-to-day running of a busy radio station. (public relations, negotiating)

1989 TO DATE Deputy G— M— RPM Radio plc – w overall resp for staffing (there are 40 f/t & up to 30 temp staff, public / staff relations & advertising. I am also involved in commissioning new progs & agreeing new prog schedules in conjunction w the G— M—.

Outside Activities wind surfing. Irish history, exotic cookery, golf

Refs Nigel Dawood
Gen Mgr
RPM Radio plc
(address from DataFiles, filename ALPHA)
page 102

Hazel Byrne
Chief Executive
SRN Network plc
(address from DataFiles, filename ALPHA)
page 102

① 1981/3
Evening Mail, Birmingham Post & Mail Group. Junior Reporter, then Reporter – the majority of this work was involved w covering local sporting & leisure events.

Key in exercise 3 (filename VITAE) for 10-pitch printout. Embolden the main heading and use the automatic centring device to centre each line. On page 2 embolden the wording after the side headings and before the dash at the beginning of the paragraphs. When you have completed this task, save under filename VITAE. Recall the document and follow the instructions for text editing on page 101.

Exercise 4

Type the following manuscript, making all corrections indicated. Please type in single spacing.

Les Femmes et la Vente sur Catalogue

L'Angleterre et l'allemagne rettrapent les Etats-Unis. La Frances voit le chiffre total des ventres par correspondence augmenter regulierement de 15% per an. Le great courant est amorce, demain la riviere sera un fleuve: qu'on le veuille ou non, la vente par correspondance est d'ores et deja un facteur important dans l'economie des pays eurpoeens a niveau de vie eleve ~~eleve~~ car le rapport pouvoir d'achat/vente par correspondance est valable partout. Et pus a l'instar ds Americans, les femmes europeennes et plus particulierement les Francaises, puisque ces sont elles qui nous occupant dans le cas present, elles aussi, ont evolue. Elles gardent evidemment et garderont toujours leur personalite nationale et les traits caracteristiques qui leur sont propres (dieu soit lout), cesci n'empeche pas qu'elles possedent sur la vie pratique de tous les jours des idees tres differentes de celles qui gouvernaient l'esprit de leurs meres il y a vingt ans. Cela parait etre une lapalikade, mais il est bon de la repeter de temps a autre car un certain nombre d'industriels francais pourtant la mission devrait etre de simplifier la vie des femmes, semble ne pas l'avoir tres bien compris.

De plus en plus, les femmes travaillent. De moins en moins, elles aiment perdre leur temps.